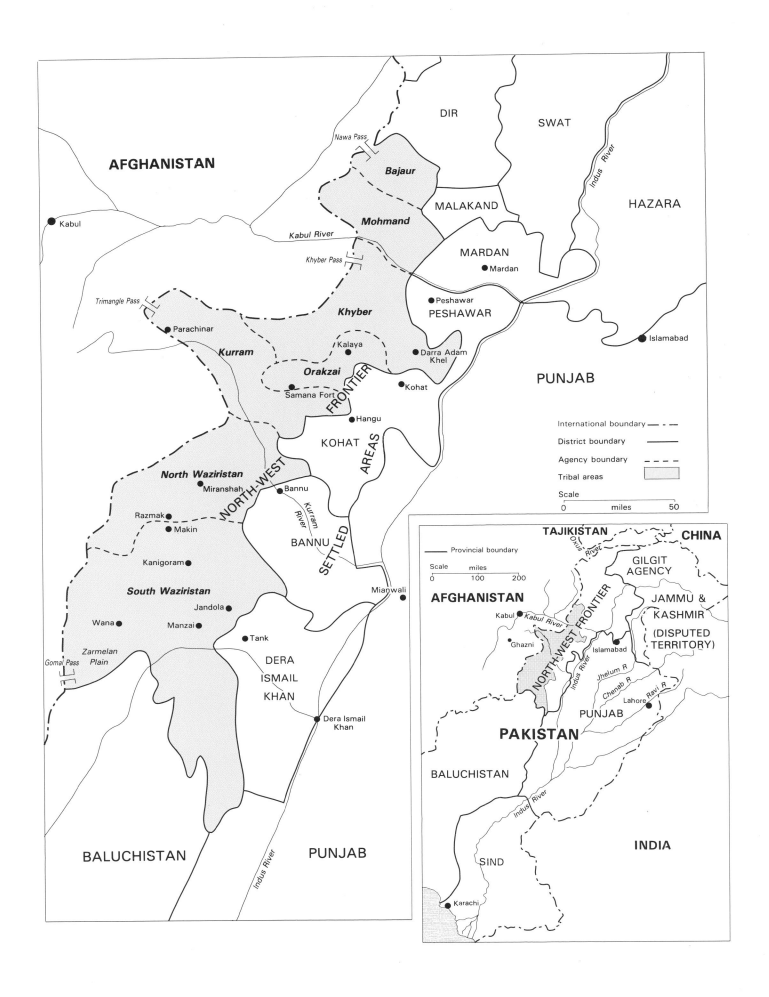

WARRIOR RACE

IMRAN KHAN

WARRIOR RACE

A journey through the land of the
Tribal Pathans

Photographs by Pervez A. Khan

Chatto & Windus
LONDON

First published 1993

1 3 5 7 9 10 8 6 4 2

First published in the United Kingdom in 1993
by Chatto & Windus Limited
Random House, 20 Vauxhall Bridge Road,
London SW1V 2SA

Random House Australia (Pty) Limited
20 Alfred Street, Milsons Point
Sydney, New South Wales 2061
Australia

Random House New Zealand Limited
18 Poland Road, Glenfield
Auckland 10, New Zealand

Random House South Africa (Pty) Limited
PO Box 337, Bergvlei, South Africa

Random House UK Limited Reg. No. 954009

A CIP catalogue record for this
book is available from the British Library

ISBN 0 7011 3890 4

Map by John Flower
Design by Margaret Sadler

Printed and Bound in Great Britain by
Butler & Tanner Ltd., Frome and London.

Contents

Introduction

MY ANCESTORS WERE Pathans from the wild and iso-
lated region of Pakistan known as the Tribal Areas,
the part of the North-West Frontier Province that
runs along the border with Afghanistan. Although
my parents and family elders instilled in me a great
pride in being a Pathan, I had never visited the tribal
heartlands until recently, when I went with a cousin,
Sohail Khan. To enter the Tribal Areas one has to get
special permission from the Pakistan government,
and very few people are actually granted this, as the
government has to provide security by way of an
armed escort. Initially I was not at all keen to visit the
area, thinking it would be a hassle to obtain the

relevant permissions, that the landscape would be mainly bare and rocky, the climate freezing in winter and boiling hot in summer, and the people hostile and uncivilized. Fortunately, Sohail persuaded me that we should visit the land of our ancestors. So, escorted by about 15 armed men, we made for Kanigoram, where a part of my mother's tribe still lives. (Her own branch of the tribe, like my father's, had come down to the greener pastures of the Punjab several centuries ago.) Kanigoram is the largest town in South Waziristan, one of the wildest and most rugged parts of the Tribal Areas.

ABOVE *Kanigoram, in South Waziristan, was the focal point of my visit to the Tribal Areas. Anyone entering the town has to negotiate this bridge.*

OPPOSITE PAGE 1 *Proud and fiercely independent, the Pathans are one of the world's greatest warrior races.*

PAGE 1 *Here I have been challenged to a shooting competition by members of my mother's tribe, the Burkis, in Kanigoram. On the right, with dark hair and dark shirt, is my cousin, Sohail Khan, whose invitation to visit the area with him led to this book.*

Nothing I had heard or read about the area matched the experience of actually being there. It is wilder than I had ever imagined any place could be. Not only is the terrain incredibly hostile, containing the most dramatic and desolate mountain ranges, but the people seem wilder than those in any Hollywood film on the Wild West I have ever seen. Unlike the cowboys, who were armed with pistols, every man here carries a rifle. Their faces are more rugged than any film cowboy's – in a country where just existing is difficult, only the tough survive. The harsh environment and the way of life have made every man a warrior.

To the outsider the Tribal Areas are lawless lands inhabited by dangerous, barbaric people who live by robbing and killing. In fact, I found completely the opposite. I was impressed by the Pathans' hospitality and politeness – so unexpected in one of the world's greatest warrior races – and most of

For me one of the attractions of the Tribal Areas was the fact that the Pathans living here have maintained their way of life for centuries. This boy is carrying a knife used for cutting grass.

3

all by their value system. It is in many ways a far more civilized society than any I have seen.

As a result of their inaccessibility, the Tribal Areas are untouched by tourism. Except on the roads, the laws of Pakistan do not apply here – the region is semi-autonomous. Tribal law prevails, and the Pathans live much as they have for centuries. Though modern communications, especially radio and television, have brought about quite a few changes in the last ten years or so, the tribes have completely preserved their laws and traditions.

I decided to write this book because I wanted to celebrate this remarkable value system. It is astonishing that in this materialistic age people can still live by a system based on honour. I wanted to capture this before modern communications bring about any major changes. I feel too that Pakistan can learn a lot from the pride the Pathans of the Tribal Areas have in their background, and the way they have preserved their customs and traditions. They have maintained their democratic system through the centuries, and every individual considers himself any man's equal – no matter how poor he is materially.

It seemed to me that the best way to prepare a book on these unique people would be to travel with a photographer through the whole tribal belt, which is divided into seven administrative regions, or agencies. Along the way I would talk to the village elders and find out what they thought of the changes in their lives. There are still many tribal elders who fought the British, and large numbers who fought to liberate Kashmir in 1947.

I began my trip in South Waziristan, the southernmost agency, and headed up through North Waziristan, Kurram, Orakzai, Khyber – the land of the Afridis – and Mohmand, finishing in the northernmost agency, Bajaur. We organized the trip through each agency's Political Agent (the Pakistan government's representative) and were accompanied by an armed escort. This was made up of Khassadars (the Political Agent's bodyguards, who are provided by the tribes that deal with a particular agent) and Scouts (especially trained police who work only in the Tribal Areas).

In order to cover the entire region, we had to make several expeditions over a period of a year. I was too busy with fund-raising for the cancer hospital in Lahore and preparations for the 1992 cricket World Cup to be able to do the

OPPOSITE ABOVE *My escort included about eight to ten Scouts (specially trained police from the Tribal Areas).*

OPPOSITE BELOW *As well as the Scouts, I was escorted by about eight Khassadars, shown here. Khassadars are armed men provided by the tribes to protect their Political Agent.*

The fortified houses and hostile terrain of North Waziristan.

trip all at one time, so, whenever I had a few days off, we resumed the journey at the point where we had broken off. Pervez Khan, the photographer, and varying numbers of Scouts and Khassadars came on every expedition. Most of the time I was also accompanied by Sohail and by my cricketer friend, Zakir Khan. (Although Pervez's and Zakir's names are Khan, they are no relation. The name Khan, which originally meant chieftain or landlord, is the most common Pathan surname.) Another friend, Dost Mohammad, a Pathan from the Mahsud tribe, who now lives in Islamabad, came with us on one occasion.

As we headed north, the scenery, the villages and, to a lesser extent, the appearance of the people changed. Waziristan was wild and harsh: the places at lower altitudes were particularly bare and rocky, while those higher up, like Kanigoram, were not quite so barren. Further north the land became greener,

ABOVE *Fruit trees blossoming in the barren South Waziristan landscape.*

PAGES 8-9 *The villages and towns of the Tribal Areas are much the same as they were centuries ago. This bazaar was in a village we visited at the base of the Trimangle Pass in Kurram.*

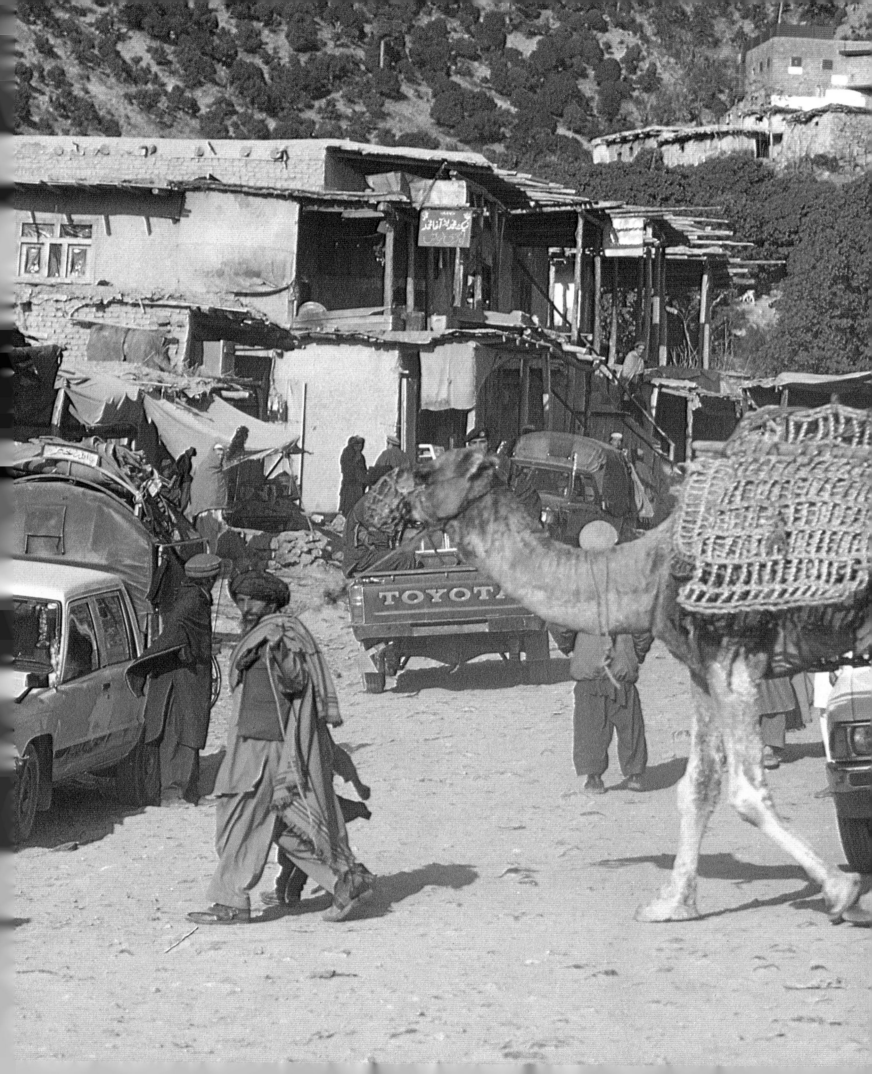

and some of the valleys were very fertile. The highlands of the northern part of the tribal belt were spectacular.

The countryside was dotted with widely dispersed villages and hamlets, each inhabited by members of a sub-tribe or clan. Most houses were built of mud. In Waziristan every house was like a fort, complete with gun towers. In Kurram Agency, however, years of relative tranquillity had resulted in an almost complete absence of gun towers – some of the houses even had verandas. We discovered that electricity had only recently reached the Tribal Areas, and only those villages that were along roads, since the roads were mainly built as a result of the Afghan war. Thus, although television had made a huge impact, it was confined to the less remote areas.

Physically, the Pathan has more in common with the people of Central Asia than with those of the subcontinent. The fine, aquiline features, high cheekbones and light skin reflect the Pathans' origins in Afghanistan and Turkey. In

A village on the Tochi River in North Waziristan. The fortified houses reflect the need for protection as a result of the prevalence of blood feuds.

South Waziristan, the Mahsuds are of medium height, lean and athletic, while in North Waziristan the Waziri tribesmen are larger but less athletic-looking. Black hair and brown eyes are the norm, but the tribesmen from the northern agencies tend to be of a slightly fairer colouring. We often came across Pathans with blue or green eyes, throughout the entire area. Many of the tribal elders dye their grey beards red with henna. In the remoter regions the traditional pagris (turbans) are worn by everyone while in more accessible areas other styles of headgear have emerged and are seen alongside the pagris.

The women of the Tribal Areas, who are principally Sunni Muslims, for the most part wear clothing in bright colours, especially red. (However, in some tribes – particularly the Orakzais, the Mohmands and even at times the Afridis – when the women reach the age of about 40, they tend to exchange the bright colours for darker, more sombre clothing.) The powindah women's clothing is even more colourful, while the Shia Muslim women, who are mainly found

Shia women in the Orakzai Tirah in their customary black clothing.
Notice how the man is ignoring them, to show respect.

11

in the Kurram Valley and the Orakzai Tirah, dress in black. None of the Pathan women wanted to be photographed.

As I got to know the Pathans' character, I recognized in it aspects of myself, particularly the competitiveness I was born with and the determination not to show fear. So often in cricket, talented young batsmen do not make the grade because they are frightened of fast bowling and being hit by the ball. But among my cousins it was unthinkable for any of us to show that we were frightened, as we would have been diminished in each other's eyes. My two older cousins, both of whom went on to captain Pakistan, were known for their courage. I had the ideal temperament for a fast bowler, as I hated being attacked by batsmen – it was the desire to strike back by bowling faster that made me develop into the first genuine fast bowler produced by my country. To avenge any type of affront is very much part of the Pathan character.

Researching the book was a pleasure, because it gave me an opportunity not only to go back to my roots but also to meet a race of people who have unusually demanding values. For example, on one occasion I met an elderly powindah (nomadic tribesman) who, with his family, was making his way back to the highlands in early spring. I asked him if I could buy the puppy he had strapped on his camel. (The powindahs' dogs are known for their intelligence and strength and make excellent watchdogs.) He replied that it was not for sale. The family had obviously not eaten for a while and had travelled a great distance, so I offered him a thousand-rupee note for the puppy. He then explained that he would not sell the dog because he had promised it to someone on the way. Even though this meant giving the dog away for nothing, he would not consider my offer of money because it would entail breaking a promise, which was unthinkable. I was so impressed by his principles that I decided to give him the money anyway. When he asked me why I was offering him money, I told him it was because he was poor and could use it. He gave me a withering look, informed me that he was not poor, and walked away, leaving me embarrassed and full of admiration.

Later on in my trip through the Tribal Areas I was to discover that this attitude was not the exception but the rule. It is the Pathan's sense of honour that makes him conduct himself with such dignity, and a fiercely independent spirit that makes even the poorest tribesman walk like a king.

OPPOSITE *The powindahs (nomadic Pathans) regard their dogs very highly and are extremely protective about them. When I tried to buy one, I discovered that they will not sell them, though they will sometimes give them as a special gift.*

CHAPTER 1

Pathan History & Culture

THE PATHANS ARE one of the world's great warrior races and yet the jirga system, upon which their society is based, is one of the oldest democratic systems known to man. To understand the Pathan psyche, it's essential to know something of the tribes' unique history and culture. There is no denying that through the centuries the Pathans have existed by raiding, robbing and kidnapping. But it was only when I entered the Tribal Areas that I realized why these people had had to adopt this way of life. In the mountainous terrain, hardly anything grows, and whatever is produced is insufficient to sustain the population of the area. Of course, there are regions where life is more comfortable than others – and where, accordingly, the incidence of lawlessness is relatively low. But on the whole, and particularly in Waziristan, life is hard. Frequently the men have been faced with the choice of either seeing their wife and children go hungry, or raiding and kidnapping from the affluent lowlands to feed them. As a result, they have often chosen to face the wrath of God, rather than the shame and disgrace of poverty. Another common stratagem was to rob traders who travelled through the passes from Central Asia to India – it was really a form of toll system.

It is not in the nature of such a proud race of people to resort to begging. As a result, robbing and kidnapping became a means of survival, which prevailed until Independence. The tribal Pathans have never considered it a crime to raid – for them, the more daring the raid, the braver the men. The Settled Areas were considered part of British India, and raiding amounted to killing two birds with one stone – fighting the British as well as bringing back booty. Raiding and looting in war was ingrained in their nature. Even now the tribal Pathan finds it hard to resist easy pickings.

Consequently, it is not surprising that to this day the government is extremely reluctant to let non-Pathan Pakistanis and, especially, foreigners enter the Tribal Areas. When I went there, my escort consisted of between 15 and 20 armed men.

PATHAN HOMELAND

Inhabited by fierce, warlike tribes, the region that became known as the North-West Frontier has always guarded the western border of the subcontinent. Nearly 2,500 years ago the Greek historian Herodotus wrote about the 'Paktuans [who] wore cloaks of skin, and carried the bow of their country and the dagger'. A century or so later, Alexander the Great, who fought four battles in Swat, remarked upon the Pathans' fierce independence.

The hilly, arid region that is now south-eastern Afghanistan and north-western Pakistan has since ancient times been the Pathans' homeland. It was only in 1893 that the British created the Durand Line separating Afghanistan from India and slicing right through the Pathans' territory. The region on the

PAGE 14 *The Durand Line separating Afghanistan from India cut right through the Pathans' homeland. This Pathan comes from Afghanistan.*

PAGE 15 *Very little grows in the bleak, rugged landscape of much of the Tribal Areas. As a result the proud and independent people turned to highway robbery and kidnapping in order to survive. These fortified houses are in North Waziristan.*

Indian side of the boundary was part of the Punjab until 1901, when Lord Curzon carved the North-West Frontier Province (NWFP) out of it. The NWFP was divided into Tribal Areas and Settled Areas at that time. In 1947 the NWFP voted to become part of the newly established country of Pakistan.

Pathans are still the predominant ethnic group in Afghanistan, and the southern population of that country is almost entirely Pathan. In Pakistan the majority of the population between the Sulaiman Mountains and the Indus River is Pathan.

Data is sparse as to when the Pathans converted to Islam or when the tribes moved into their present areas. My father's tribe, the Niazis, trace their descent back about a thousand years to Niaz Khan, the second son of Ibrahim Lodhi; he was the son of Shah Hussain, the King of Ghor in Afghanistan. The Niazis were pushed out from near Ghazni in Afghanistan around the 13th century by the larger Ghilzai tribe. They settled along the west bank of the Indus River, from Tank to Bannu. At this time the Burkis, my mother's tribe, predominated in Waziristan, having come down from Afghanistan two centuries before.

The Yusufzai tribe moved into the Vale of Peshawar and Swat, while the Marwats and Khattaks, as well as the Niazis, occupied the fertile plains on the banks of the Indus. Other tribes or parts of tribes went much further into India. A section of the Burkis became landowners in the fertile 'Doab', the land between the Sutlej and Beas rivers. There were Pathan settlements in Northern India in Hoshiarpur, Pathankot, near Lukhnow, Rohailkand and many other areas.

Nearer the Tribal Areas, the tribes living on the more productive plains were constantly under pressure from those in the mountains. Stronger tribes have relentlessly encroached on the land of weaker ones. Waziri and Mahsud raids extended right down to Mianwali and Isa Khel on the Indus. Bannu was raided by the Waziris, and Tank by the Mahsuds during the British raj. The Afridis raided Peshawar earlier this century.

One pattern emerges quite clearly. When their numbers grew to a point where the unproductive terrain could not support any more people, the more enterprising tribes would attack and occupy the plains to the east. In desperation, a tribe would look for greener pastures in the lowlands, or subsections of the tribe would move to the lowlands to seek employment in the police or army or even to start trading. The movement of Pathan tribes from tribal areas to the fertile and prosperous lowlands corresponded to the weakness of the Indian kingdoms: whenever there was a power vacuum, the hungrier and tougher mountain tribes would seize the opportunity.

17

For example, in the mid 16th century, when the Yusufzai leader Khan Kaju defeated the Ghawanak Khel tribe at the battle of Sheikh Tapur, it opened the way for the Khattaks to move eastwards and the Afridis to occupy the Tirah region. Similarly, in Waziristan in the 17th century, when the Burkis were weakened by migration to India, the Mahsud encroachment on their territory commenced; they are now left with only the territory around the town of Kanigoram. The Waziris and Bitanis are constantly having to protect their lands from the fierce Mahsud tribe.

Until about 20 years ago, the southern tribal Pathans wore their hair in a shoulder-length bob, spoke the soft dialect of Pushtu and still performed tribal dances. They went into battle dancing to the beat of the drum, which functioned as the standard of the tribe. The northern Pathans shaved their heads, spoke the hard dialect, did not dance and fought battles under the tribal standard.

Within their own areas the tribal Pathans lead a semi-nomadic existence. In the summer they move up into the highlands, and in the winter they come down to the valleys. Over the past century the more affluent members of the tribe have acquired winter homes in the cities of the Settled Areas. Wealthy Mahsuds have houses in Tank and Dera Ismail Khan, Waziris in Bannu and Miranshah, and Afridis and neighbouring tribes like Mohmands in Peshawar. They have no problem adapting to the mountainous terrain after city life, but it has inevitably meant that these affluent tribesmen have become less hardy than they used to be. One tribal malik (an influential member of the tribe) told me that he preferred to bring up his children in the mountains, as they grew up to be much stronger.

A COMMON ANCESTRY

Pathans believe they are all descended from a common ancestor, Qais. He is said to have met the prophet of Islam, Muhammad, who lived from about 570 until 632. The prophet gave Qais the name 'P'thun', and Qais was to take Islam back to his home. One of Qais's sons was Afghana, who had four sons. Every Pathan tribe traces its descent from one of these four sons.

The first of these four Pathan branches is the Sarbani; this includes the largest Pathan tribe, the Yusufzai, which settled in the Swat area, as well as the Tarkalani, Mohmands and Muhammadzai. The second grouping is the Bitani. My father's tribe, the Niazis, belongs to this branch, along with the Ghilzais (one of the largest Pathan tribes in Afghanistan), Lodhis, Suris, Marwats, Lohanis, Bitanis and Nuhranis. The third branch is the Karlani, which includes some of the wildest tribes, such as the Mahsud, Waziri, Afridi,

Boys sharpening their hunting instincts with catapults, as they are too young to afford guns.

Orakzai, Dawar and Bangash. The majority of Pathan tribes living in the Tribal Areas are from this branch. The last grouping is the Ghurghushti, of which the Shinwari are in the Tribal Areas, and the other tribes in the Baluchistan region south of the NWFP.

AN INDEPENDENT NATURE

Little is known of the Pathans' history until Mahmud of Ghazni, the king of what was to become Afghanistan, led an invasion into India nearly 1000 years ago. For 1500 years before his arrival, the kingdom of Gandhara had been centred on the Vale of Peshawar. It is remembered principally for its Buddhist art, which along with some ruins is all that remains of the civilization. Mahmud conquered the area and gradually the people began to be converted to Islam. His army was made up mainly of Pathans. It was during his raids on Somnath that the Burkis, my mother's tribe, first made history, leading the assault on the famous Hindu temple of Somnath (see page 55).

Through the centuries, Pathan tribes have resisted all conquerors. Their

The ruins of the Buddhist monastery at Takht-i-Bahi, built around 2000 years ago. Buddhist ruins and art are all that is left of the kingdom of Gandhara.

fiercely independent nature has made it impossible for any empire or conqueror to subdue them for any length of time. Yet the Pathans' independent spirit has proved a double-edged sword. Although enabling them to retain their freedom throughout history, it has also prevented them from building empires of their own.

Various Pathan kingdoms were established in Delhi. In the mid 15th century, during what is known as the Sultanate period, the Lodhi dynasty ruled for a short time. The Lodhis were joined by their cousin tribes, the Suris and the Niazis, who were given estates in return for providing fighting men to help maintain the Lodhi empire. The Lodhi dynasty actually had more problems dealing with the Pathan aristocracy than it did in resisting external threats to its kingdom. Every Pathan tribal malik considered himself an equal of the sultan, and the slightest discourtesy or affront by the sultan could lead to a rebellion. It was a disenchanted group of Pathans that invited Babur to topple their own Lodhi kingdom in 1526; his victory at the Battle of Panipat marked the beginning of the Moghul Empire, which was to rule the subcontinent for the next two and a half centuries.

There was a brief interlude when India was again brought under Pathan rule, after the great Sher Shah Suri defeated Babur's son, the emperor Humayun, in 1539. But although Sher Shah Suri became the head of the entire Pathan nation through his tremendous leadership qualities, it did not mean that his sons were going to be accepted as kings too. In fact, the Suri reign collapsed because it was weakened by the civil war that followed Sher Shah Suri's death. The Pathans became so fragmented that the Moghuls, under Humayun, were able to recapture the throne from them. The Pathans never again held an empire in India – though they provided princes, governors, generals and fighters for various kingdoms in the subcontinent.

PATHAN RESISTANCE TO THE MOGHULS

During the reign of Akbar, Humayun's son, the Moghul empire had to contend with a revolt led by the first Pathan nationalist, Pir E Roshan. My grandmother was descended from him. (Pir E Roshan's real name was Bayazid Khan – 'pir' means 'saint'). More or less all of the Tribal Areas were behind the pir. One reason for the revolt was that the Pathans, as strict Muslims, could not tolerate the version of Islam upheld by Akbar (as set out in his book *Din E Elahi*). Pir E Roshan believed that Akbar was a heretic and that it was the duty of Pathans to jihad (undertake a holy war) against him. A second reason was that Pir E Roshan was a descendant of Aba Shahbaz, who had married the daughter of the king of Herat. Because the king of Herat was

considered to be of older and nobler royal blood than the Moghuls, Pir E Roshan felt that he had a right to rule, rather than the Moghul Akbar, whose grandfather had in any case illegally taken the Hindustan empire from the Lodhi Pathans.

Pir E Roshan fought the Moghuls, and after him his six sons carried on the struggle. All but one of the sons died fighting them. The remaining son, Jallaluddin, was killed by the Hazaras, a tribe on the Indus. (In one of Akbar's expeditions against Jallaluddin, a Niazi force assisted the Moghuls, fighting fellow Pathans.) Pir E Roshan too was killed, and his head was buried in Kanigoram. His daughter-in-law, Bibi Alai, carried on the struggle, eventually came to terms with the Moghuls and was given estates near Jallandar.

The Roshanniyya Movement, as this Pathan rebellion was known, persisted into the 17th century. Its leader, Ahadad Khan, nephew of Pir E Roshan, became the Pathan leader and inflicted several defeats on the Moghuls. At Katakushta, near Ali Masjid, the army of the Moghul governor was ambushed and destroyed. The governor fled, deserting his wife and daughter, who, as a result, chose to stay with the Pathans even though they were free to leave. Ahadad was supported in this battle by the Afridis and Orakzais, who later

Scouts being served tea at the officers' mess, Wana cantonment. Built by the British in the late 19th century as part of their defence of the North-West Frontier, Wana cantonment was attacked by a combined force of Waziris and Mahsuds led by the Waziristan hero Mullah Powindah.

helped him to defeat the Moghuls again, on the Gunahgara Plain near the mountains of Tirah. To the last days of the Moghuls, Pathans never stopped harassing the Moghul armies in the North-West Frontier. The Moghuls' fighting strength was sapped by these rebellions, and their supply of fresh fighting stock from among the tribes of Central Asia (including Pathan tribes, many of whom cooperated with the Moghuls) was drastically reduced.

During the 18th century, as the Moghuls gradually lost control of the subcontinent, the Sikhs became the masters of Punjab, and it was not long before they came into confrontation with the Pathans. Although for a while they managed to control the plains, the Sikhs were never able to establish any kind of authority in the tribal highlands. They suffered a major defeat when their great general, Hari Singh, who was fighting the Pathans at Jamrud, was killed by the forces of the Afghan general, Akbar Khan.

THE GREAT GAME

By the middle of the 19th century the British had become the masters of the subcontinent. Their initial contact with the Pathans was during the first Afghan War (1838-42). Britain, concerned about a possible Russian invasion of its Indian empire via the North-West Frontier, wanted to make the region a buffer state under British influence and warned Russia not to tamper with the boundaries of Afghanistan. This marked the beginning of the so-called Great Game, characterized by espionage and intrigue, which dominated British policy in the Tribal Areas for the second half of the 19th century. To allow the movement of troops into Afghanistan and to defend the border, the British had to secure the mountain passes. When they attempted to occupy the passes and build forts and roads, they came into contact with the tribal Pathans – who saw all this as an attempt to take away their independence.

The British did not fully understand the sort of people they were dealing with. They tried the carrot-and-stick policy: giving subsidies to the tribes to keep the roads safe, and at the same time sending military expeditions to punish them when they misbehaved. Yet despite putting blockades on tribes, bombing them, destroying their precious fruit trees, even throwing salt on their cultivated land, the British were never able to subjugate the Pathans. The tribes maintained their independence, though at a great cost.

PAGES 24-25 *A landscape in Kurram. The concrete-and-mud spikes that look like sandcastles were devised in the early 20th century by the British, who controlled the Kurram Valley; they and were intended to prevent Russian tanks from invading.*

(Over a century later, the Russians had much the same problem, when they discovered that even superior technology is not enough against a race prepared to fight to the end for its freedom. Out of Afghanistan's population of 14 million, over a million gave their lives to keep their country independent after the Soviet invasion of 1979. In the end, even a recognized superpower of its time had to withdraw against a race that has faith and is too proud to accept slavery.)

THE PATHAN PSYCHE

An incident occurred early in the 20th century that I think explains the workings of the Pathan mind, and the inability of the British to understand it. I was told of it by a friend, Muzzafar Khan Afridi. His father had known the Pathan concerned, a young Afridi called Sher Khan. Sher Khan had moved to Peshawar from Tirah with his family. He had found a job, but it kept him away from his home for days. One day when he came back he found some evidence that his wife was seeing another man. In a rage he killed her and the man with whom he believed she was having an affair. The British found him guilty of murder. Despite his explanation that under tribal law he was within his rights, he was sentenced to life imprisonment in the Andaman Islands.

The prison warders were bemused by Sher Khan. A tall, handsome man with a noble bearing, he stood apart from the other criminals, who looked upon him with awe – not least because of his immense physical strength. Gradually it became apparent to everyone that Sher Khan did not belong there. He was given increasingly responsible tasks and considerable freedom, and his sentence was reduced to five years. But then a year before he was due to be released, a top British officer came on a tour of the island – and Sher Khan suddenly jumped on the officer and killed him.

Everyone was amazed at his stupidity, but Sher Khan was unrepentant. He felt that according to the Pathan code of honour he had been in the right in killing his wife and her supposed lover to protect the honour of his family, especially his children. Life was no substitute for the dishonour of being treated as an ordinary criminal; he felt he had to avenge the great injustice that had been done to him, and the British officer was the only one upon whom he could take his revenge. In the end Sher Khan was hanged.

THE KIDNAPPING OF MOLLY ELLIS

Another incident, which happened at around the same time, became a cause célèbre in India and Britain. In the 1920s the British accused an Adam Khel Afridi named Ajab Khan of stealing rifles. With a small force they searched Ajab's village, where they made the mistake of also searching Ajab's house.

The rumour went round that Ajab's wife was searched as well. When Ajab returned, his wife demanded vengeance and he planned revenge in the true Pathan way. Ajab decided to kidnap the major's daughter, Molly Ellis, and in the ensuing struggle on the veranda of their bungalow in Kohat the girl's mother was killed. Ajab took the young girl with him to Tirah. There was a tremendous amount of British outrage, and various attempts were made to find Ajab and Molly. Eventually he gave her up, unmolested, and then crossed the border into Afghanistan, where he was hailed as a national hero.

THE MALIKI SYSTEM

Before the arrival of the British, the Tribal Areas were fragmented. The British resolved to deal directly with the tribes. The system Britain introduced in the Tribal Areas was the Maliki system, whereby the tribes' maliks, or most influential members, were paid allowances. The British tried to strengthen the maliks in order to wield power through them, as they had done successfully in the rest of the subcontinent, where they strengthened existing monarchies,

The Pathans of Pakistan's Tribal Areas and southern Afghanistan have always had close links, and along the border there are many signs of the recent Afghan War. These are Mujahideen guerrillas' graves in the Trimangle Pass.

feudal landlords and chiefs who would obey them. Even in Baluchistan, where the tribes were warlike and tough, the hierarchical tribal system meant that the British could wield power through the sardar (leader), who had great loyalty from his tribe. (What the United States is doing in the Muslim world today is very similar. Because it is much more convenient to deal with friendly dictators than with democracies, dictatorships are encouraged and patronized throughout the Islamic countries at the cost of democracy. Algeria is a classic example.)

This policy failed in the Tribal Areas, however, because the maliks had little influence over their tribesmen, who continually disowned maliks they perceived as British agents and instead threw up leaders seen to have the tribal interest at heart. The policy did work occasionally in the northern tribal belt, but it usually depended upon the capabilities of the individual Political Agent (government representative).

In Waziristan it created chaos. The first Political Agent of Waziristan was astonished to see almost 3000 Mahsuds turn up at the jirga, or tribal council. They all considered themselves maliks. In one of the Mahsud jirgas he held, a tribesman, by the name of Jagger, Abdur Rahman Khel Bhalolzai, stood up and declared, 'Let it be "field" [battlefield] and blow us all up with cannon, or make all 18,000 of us nawabs [feudal lords].' Nevertheless, the system still exists, because there has never been a concerted effort to evolve a better one.

The malik is extremely sensitive to his people's wishes. Unlike a feudal lord, who imposes his will upon a servile population, the malik takes great pains to make the people remember that he is one of them. Individuals within the tribe are highly independent and well aware of their rights. Rarely will a malik pass a piece of legislation that is unpopular. In 1890 a few Mahsud maliks who were thought not to be representing the tribal interests were assassinated.

In fact, any powerful man who tries to misuse his power on weaker members of the tribe is liable to be punished. One of the tribal elders of the Burkis in Kanigoram, Pir Yacub Shah Danishmandi, told me that he had known at least three men whose houses had been burnt down by the whole tribe because each had been cruel and unjust to a weaker opponent. On one occasion a man was publicly executed.

THE FCR SYSTEM

After the British failed in the political subjugation of the tribes through the Maliki system, they came up with a new approach, which is still in use today. This FCR (Frontier Crimes Regulation) system is based on the tribal law system. (Tribal criminal justice is rooted in Islamic tradition and is in many ways similar to that of the Bedouin tribes. The aim is to satisfy the aggrieved party, whereas Western law seeks to punish the guilty.)

The first aspect of the system stipulates that when a crime (either civil or criminal) occurs, the Political Agent asks the jirga to conduct an enquiry to determine who is guilty and why, and then to recommend a punishment. The Political Agent will never go against the recommendations of the jirga. For instance, if the jirga decides that a murderer should only be fined, the Political Agent cannot pass a death sentence.

The second part of the FCR system provides for the punishment of the entire sub-tribe. In other words, when a crime is committed within the jurisdiction of a sub-tribe, the whole sub-tribe is seen as defaulting, and the government is entitled to imprison as many members as it can lay its hands on, releasing them only after the tribe has paid a fine. This part of the system is detested by the tribes – but according to the Political Agents, if it were not for this threat, it would be impossible to control the tribes.

TRIBAL LAWS AND CUSTOMS

Since 1947, when Pakistan gained its independence from Britain, and the North-West Frontier Province voted to become part of Pakistan, the Pakistan government has followed the British example in dealing with the tribes. The Tribal Areas, consisting of seven agencies and four Frontier Regions (which are attached to the districts of Dera Ismail Khan, Bannu, Kohat and Peshawar), have been allowed to remain more or less autonomous regions, governed by their own laws.

On the roads, the law of Pakistan applies – the government, like its predecessors the British, actually pays allowances to the tribes to keep the roads open. But everywhere else, tribal law prevails. Out of about 600 federal laws of Pakistan, only 44 apply in the Tribal Areas, and none of these directly affects the lives of the Pathans. The government's representative in each agency, the Political Agent, deals with the tribes through their jirgas. It is therefore a unique situation – the existence of a part of a country in which the government has virtually no authority. If a man commits a crime and then goes into the Tribal Areas, the government can do nothing except to request that the tribe hand him over.

The tribes live by their own laws and customs. Every man can carry a gun without a licence, which makes the area seem rather like the American Wild West. If someone is killed in a feud, it is up to the jirga to deal with the situation. The only time the government interferes is when an incident takes place on the roads. Even then, it approaches the tribal jirga; there is no direct action.

In the Tribal Areas every man can carry a gun. This North Waziristan tribesman carries his trusted 303, which used to be the most sought-after rifle. Today the preferred gun in most areas is the Kalashnikov.

The government rarely gives permission for foreigners or non-Pathan Pakistanis to visit the Tribal Areas. If anyone is kidnapped or robbed, the government has to go through the elaborate procedure of calling a tribal jirga to hand over the person or stolen goods. In these circumstances, the jirga usually gets some concessions from the government in return. At times a tribe will kidnap someone just for the leverage it gives them with the Political Agent, since the release of the person will procure some favour from the agent.

Very recently six Chinese nationals were kidnapped by a Pathan tribe to obtain government concessions. My cousin, Jamshed Burki, who is an expert in tribal dealings, led the negotiations for their release.

THE JIRGA SYSTEM

The tribal society is run by the jirga system. One of the oldest democratic systems in the world, it has been described as 'the closest thing to Athenian democracy that has existed since the original'. The respected elders and maliks of the tribe get together and by consensus take decisions for the tribe. The

The jirga system is the basis of tribal society. The jirga takes decisions for the tribe, passes legislation and decides punishments for crimes. This is a jirga of the Sulaiman Khel tribe in South Waziristan. Notice that it is the elders who are given the seats. They also dominate the discussions – age is associated with wisdom, and the elders are accorded great respect.

jirga, or council, passes legislation on tribal disputes, dealings with the government, murder cases and so on. It can award fines or death sentences or banish people from the tribe.

A sub-tribe will generally have a jirga of around ten men, but a jirga can be made up of anywhere from five men to around two thousand. It is the jirga system that has enabled the Pathans to remain unconquered, because it has been impossible for a conqueror to deal with any one person; he has had to deal with the entire tribe. (Indeed, the only times a tribe has become absolutely united have been when its independence has been threatened by an outsider.) And even if the tribe has been subdued temporarily, there have been individuals who have continued to conduct guerrilla warfare.

REPRESENTATION IN PARLIAMENT
The maliks of an area choose the area's Member of Parliament, though, sadly, these days this system has degenerated into a situation whereby the richest malik often simply buys the votes of the other maliks in order to get into Parliament. The government dispenses funds for the area through the Member of

The Afghan War led to increased arms trafficking, though production of weaponry has always been a thriving industry in the Tribal Areas. Despite crude machinery, the gunsmiths' workmanship is excellent.

Parliament, which opens up a number of opportunities for him to make more money.

It is an unsatisfactory system, and most of the younger tribesmen feel it is outdated. They want adult franchise so that they can choose the man who is most likely to represent their interests in Parliament. At present, there is a debate going on in the Tribal Areas about adult franchise and doing away with the present system. The Political Agents generally argue that if the system is changed, then even the jirga system could break down, leading to anarchy and complete lawlessness. Somehow, I don't think this is likely to happen. I believe that the tribal traditions are too strong for the jirga system to break down, and I feel there should be adult franchise. There is no doubt, however, that with more money flowing into the Tribal Areas as a result of tribal Pathans working in the Gulf and in Karachi, the maliks and the jirgas do not wield as much power as they used to.

Growing affluence in the Tribal Areas has also been due to the increased trafficking in arms, as a result of the recent Afghan War, and, in some areas, drugs, especially heroin and, to a lesser extent, opium. (Opium has been traditionally used by tribal Pathans during war to give stamina and energy.)

A CODE OF HONOUR

The word 'Pathan' is a distortion of the word 'Pukhtun'. Broken down, this word means 'backbone (loyalty), hospitality, bravery and honour'. The Pathan culture is based around these principles, which are enshrined in a code of honour known as pukhtunwali, or 'the way of the Pathans'. A Pathan is recognized by other Pathans not so much by racial characteristics as by his adherence to pukhtunwali. If he does not follow the code, he is not a Pathan. And the wilder the tribes, the more strictly they adhere to the code of honour.

Pukhtunwali is closely linked to the spirit of Islamic justice and rejection of unfairness. The criterion by which a man is judged is not the amount of money he has but how honourable he and his family are. To maintain his honour a Pathan will go to any lengths. Any slight to his honour has to be avenged – there is no question of turning the other cheek. If a member of the family is murdered, his death has to be avenged, no matter how long it takes. If a woman in the family has been insulted, then, until the insult has been dealt with, the family's honour is at stake. Revenge is taken only on the male members of a family; it is considered cowardly to hurt the females.

This insistence upon revenge may be repellent to the Western mind, but it does serve as a great deterrent. A man in a rage may think twice before beating up or even murdering another man if he knows that it would inevitably lead to

a blood feud imperilling his family and himself. Hence, more crime is committed in a few weeks in Peshawar or other cities of the Settled Areas than in the whole of the Tribal Areas in a year – despite every man being armed.

The women in the family will demand revenge as much as the male members, even if it means risking the life of their men. They realize that their children's marriage prospects and their futures will depend upon how honourable the rest of the tribe believes the family to be.

It is this trait in a tribal Pathan's character that makes him such a dangerous enemy. Time is unimportant – he will wait until the right moment, when he is completely ready, even if it takes years. It often happens that if a boy's father has been killed, his mother will prepare him for taking revenge when he is old enough. There was a case in Tirah in the 1870s where the tail of a horse belonging to an Afridi tribesman's guest was cut off as a joke by the tribesman's cousins. So furious was he at the insult to his guest that he shot both cousins. That sparked off a blood feud which a century later had claimed over a hundred lives.

PATHAN HOSPITALITY

This example brings me to another important aspect of the Pathan character – hospitality. Anyone going to the Tribal Areas expecting barbarism will be shocked by the level of hospitality. Given the scarce resources in the area, the feasts that are laid for the guests are astonishing. One of my friends, who comes from Waziristan, once invited me to visit his village, about 30 kilometres north of Wana, adding that because I would be his guest he too would eat well for a few days. Indeed, a guest will be given food even if the host's family goes without.

The guest will also be protected completely. Anyone who becomes the guest of a tribal Pathan can rest assured that only over the host's dead body would any harm come to him. There have actually been incidents where an enemy, when he has walked into a man's house, has been treated the same as any guest and even given protection. It is the Pathan's duty to offer sanctuary to anyone seeking it, including criminals – and a lot of criminals live in the Tribal Areas, under the protection of the tribes. In return, they have to earn their keep, becoming helpers on farms, or even guards of their hosts, and are thus dependent upon the tribes. In Khyber Agency I met a Niazi who had escaped from

OPPOSITE *Blood feuds dominate life in much of the Tribal Areas. This Sulaiman Khel boy from a village on the Zarmelan Plain has become the head of his family, following the death of his father, who was killed in a blood feud. His father was a malik and the boy has inherited the position.*

Mianwali, having been convicted of murder, and who was living with Afridi tribesmen. He swore he was innocent and had been framed, but, sadly, there was nothing I could do to help him.

When I was travelling around the Tribal Areas, I was the guest of the Political Agents, who worried about my going to certain areas which they felt were not safe. But once I got to know the people I realized how unnecessary was the agents' concern. The people who were robbed or kidnapped – usually members of other tribes, traders laden with goods, or affluent foreigners – were chosen carefully. Television arrived in the Tribal Areas in the past decade, so most people knew of me and were extremely hospitable. They took great pride in me, regarding me as one of them. Wherever I went I was given a great welcome and invited to stay.

I was amazed by the degree of courtesy and politeness Pathans from different tribes accorded each other. It did not matter if one was a malik and the other was relatively poor – they would treat each other as equals and with respect. (This is in sharp contrast to the rest of the subcontinent, where as a result of centuries of feudal system a person from a higher social stratum may treat someone from a lower one as inferior.) Even the servants in Pathan households are treated as family members. In Mianwali, my father's village on the banks of the Indus near the NWFP border, the female servants were called Auntie and the male servants Uncle by the children.

PRESERVING THE TRIBAL VALUES

I found that the wilder the tribes, the more strictly they follow the code of honour, pukhtunwali. It is adhered to by the Pathans in the Settled Areas too, though not as rigidly. Once Pathans are out of the tribal system, however, they gradually adapt to the customs of the place where they live. My mother's branch of the Burki tribe, which broke away from the Tribal Areas over 300 years ago, continued to follow the code of honour because they lived in a tribal system, in settlements known as bastis outside the Indian town of Jallandar. But at Partition in 1947 they migrated to Lahore and other towns in the Punjab and became scattered, and gradually their Pathan characteristics have begun to disappear.

I remember that, as I was growing up, if I got into a fight with my Burki cousins, they were not as bent upon avenging a blow as my Niazi cousins (from my father's side). The Niazis still live as a tribe in Isa Khel and Mianwali districts (although due to better communications they too have lost many of their Pathan traits). When I was a boy, the period after the harvest was the time when scores were settled in Mianwali district. Money from the harvest was

used to purchase arms, and hostilities were resumed. The Mianwali district had the highest murder rate in Pakistan until the 1970s.

The Burkis living in the Punjab have assimilated more with the Punjabis in the half-century or so since Partition than they did in 300 years before Partition. They never used to marry outside their tribe; if someone did so, it was hard to marry their children back into the Burkis. Now things are getting more relaxed, but I hope that both the Niazis and the Burkis do not lose their pride in their heritage.

GOING TO EXTREMES

Throughout my travels in the Tribal Areas there were certain traits in the people that stood out (although ultimately it is difficult to generalize about their character since they are so fiercely independent and individualistic).

The worst aspect was their lack of emphasis on education. This is particularly sad because they are an enterprising race and are not realizing their full potential. In the past they have resisted education in order to preserve their

Hospitality is enshrined in pukhtunwali, the Pathan code of honour. Here, in the Kurram Valley, we are being entertained in the hujra, or part of a home reserved for men. My host is the elder in the centre.

37

independence. Yet in the Qur'an the most frequently occurring word, after the names of Allah, is education. I am sure that if the Pathans realized the great emphasis placed on education in Islam, they would take to it with the same zeal as they place on following their religion.

The Pathans are a people of extremes. As the Pathan poet Ghani Khan puts it, 'They make the most loyal friends and at the same time the deadliest enemies. Though great fighters, they make bad soldiers, as they hate taking orders. They have kindness in their character, yet hate showing it as it may be taken as a sign of weakness. Despite being poor they have remained proud.'

I discovered during my days in the Tribal Areas that it is a Pathan's deep love of freedom and his respect for the dignity of the individual that have made him tolerate physical hardship in order to preserve his value system. A Pathan boy is told by his parents and tribal elders about courage, glory, death, war, pride and above all ghairath (honour). He is shown that these are more important than life itself, so that he does not mind killing or dying. Every Pathan considers himself a king, hence the constant struggle between cousins, brothers, even at times fathers and sons.

RELIGIOUS ZEAL

The tribal Pathan observes every instruction of the Qur'an with great zeal. When travelling, according to the Qur'an, a Muslim needs to say prayers only once a day, instead of the usual five times. Yet our escort of Scouts and Khassadars would insist on stopping whenever it was the time to pray; they didn't care that the Qur'an had actually made allowance for people who were travelling. On one occasion, when my photographer, Pervez Khan, was not praying with us (as he was exercising the leniency allowed by the Qur'an when travelling), a tribesman took me aside and enquired if he was really a Muslim.

There has been only one known instance of a Pathan converting to Christianity. It was at the time of the British raj, when a missionary converted a young Pathan boy in Bannu. When the boy's father found out, he was so furious that he came down to Bannu and killed the missionary.

Growing up in such a harsh environment, the Pathans are complete fatalists, because of their total faith in Islam. They feel that the world is a transitory place and that if you live like a true Muslim there is nothing to worry about. Also, they follow the Islamic saying that if you are afraid of man, you are not in

OPPOSITE *From the cradle a Pathan boy is taught the importance of honour and bravery. Some boys inherit guns at an early age due to the wealth of their father – or his untimely death.*

awe of God (ie have no faith in God) and if you have faith in God you are not afraid of man. As a result of the strength of their beliefs, the Pathans have followed holy men in war. Nowhere in the world have so many mullahs, pirs and faqirs been so much in the forefront of fighting. From my grandmother's ancestor, Pir E Roshan, right down to the faqir of Ippi (see page 66), the religious men have led the tribesmen into battle against what they have perceived as unfairness or a threat to their independence.

Even now, after the victory of the Mujahideen, the new Afghan government is strongly Islamic. When I read that Gulbuddin Hekmatyar is a fundamentalist and that members of other Afghan Mujahideen groups are moderates, I wonder if anyone has bothered to find out the religious views of the moderates. As far as I could see from my travels in the Tribal Areas, all the Pathans are strict Muslims and are extremely religious.

My first visit to the Tribal Areas coincided with the month of fasting. My cousin, Sohail Khan, who had a stomach ulcer and was advised by his doctor to eat and drink regularly, found it impossible to get anything to eat or drink from sunrise to sunset. He was too embarrassed to ask anyone, as it is not in a Pathan's psyche to understand that a doctor has ordered someone not to fast. Even though the Qur'an allows a Muslim to forgo fasting if he is ill or travelling, the tribal Pathan feels that this law applies only to sissies. So poor Sohail Khan was forced to fast with us. (As we were travelling long distances, the lack of sustenance was quite testing. Pervez Khan would become useless by the afternoon, and I frequently found him dozing rather than concentrating on taking photographs. I constantly had to remind him of the powindahs, who would walk all day in the hot sun while fasting.)

SOCIAL SECURITY SYSTEM

One of the most remarkable aspects of tribal life is the 'social security' system. Although Pathans are continually competing with one another, they will always come to the aid of fellow tribesmen in need. On the way to Waziristan I had a firsthand experience of the extent to which tribesmen will help each other. Our jeep had got stuck while crossing a stream – some water had got into the engine. We would have been stuck there for ages had not a truck come by. The drivers were Mahsuds, as was my companion, Dost Mohammad, and the moment they learned this they began to help us. I was astonished at the lengths they went to. They spent hours inspecting the engine, and then in the end produced ropes to pull the jeep out. After that they towed us for about 50 kilometres to the town of Tank, where we had the jeep fixed.

The same system applies when tribesmen leave the Tribal Areas. For

instance, Dost Mohammad told me how when Mahsuds go to work in such places as Karachi or the Middle East, they are helped by other Mahsuds living there. They are provided with shelter and food until they can find a job and stand on their own feet, and they are given contacts to help them find work.

In Karachi I once met a Mahsud tribesman who was running a shop. I asked him how he had happened to leave the Tribal Areas and why he chose Karachi to live. He told me that he was one of the younger members of a large family, whose resources were not enough for all of them to live comfortably. He had left to seek work, but, unable to afford a train ticket to Karachi, he had ridden illegally, been thrown off twice and ended up in jail after fighting a ticket inspector. Upon being released he again got on the train, eventually reaching Karachi. At first the only work he was able to obtain was difficult manual labour and he was paid hardly enough to feed himself. After a couple of weeks, he had learnt enough Urdu to get by and at the same time to explore the sprawling city of nine million people. By chance he came across a couple of Waziri tribesmen, working as lorry drivers. Straightaway they introduced him

Pathans are devout Muslims. These men are praying while the children play nearby. It is the men who look after the children, while the women work. Note the weapons which are never far from reach.

41

to the Pathan fraternity in Karachi, found him a more lucrative job and put him up until he had made enough money to find himself a place. After a year he invited his two brothers to join him, and they set up their own trading business, helped by fellow tribesmen.

Karachi these days has a Pathan population of over two million, more than any other city in Pakistan. The initiative of the tribesmen is remarkable. From the toughest manual labour they graduate within a few years to trading. The transport industry in Karachi, and indeed most of Pakistan, is in the hands of the tribesmen.

According to this Mahsud tribesman, when he arrived in Karachi, the city people considered him simple. Later on he discovered that being forthright and straightforward – the norm in the Tribal Areas – was interpreted in the city as lack of intelligence. Thus, as well as a language barrier (the Pathans speak principally Pushtu and the city people Urdu) the tribesmen have to contend with a fundamental lack of understanding of their basic character.

Also, without the tribal customs, they are thoroughly confused by city life for a while. Whereas lying is a disgrace in the Tribal Areas, in the city the Pathans are faced with deceit and crime all round them. On top of this there are taxes, customs, government systems, corrupt policemen, none of which they have come across before. Some cannot cope with it and turn to crime, as fighting comes naturally to Pathans and there is no tribal code there to hold them back. Were it not for the support they receive from their fellow tribesmen when they have their initial exposure to city life, they would be in desperate straits. This cooperation occurs not just in Karachi but in other cities too. For example, when members of my father's tribe, the Niazis, went to Lahore, fellow tribesmen always helped them find jobs. My father was instrumental in settling a few Niazi families in Lahore in the 1950s and '60s.

SELFLESSNESS AND PRACTICALITY

Although the Pathan believes in honour above all, he also has a very deep-rooted practical streak. This unusual combination of traits is particularly apparent in a Yusufzai custom that persisted until the 1930s (although from the mid 19th century it had begun to diminish). The Yusufzai, in order to maintain their fighting qualities and toughness and at the same time an element of fairness, would share their fertile land. Every five years the members of the tribe who possessed the fertile lowlands would give them up to those members of the tribe who had been subsisting on the tougher highlands. I don't know if there is any precedent for this custom elsewhere in the world, but it seemed an incredible combination of selflessness and pragmatism.

CRICKET AMONG PATHANS

When I watched cricket matches in the Tribal Areas, their competitiveness reminded me of Zaman Park, my home in Lahore. This area of the city where my cousins and I grew up was named after my grandfather's brother, Ahmad Zaman. Although there were only about ten houses around Zaman Park, the standard of sport there was extraordinary. Whether we played cricket or hockey, no game was complete without being interrupted by fights, such was the level of aggression and competitiveness. When we played as a team against outsiders it was war.

I remember that other clubs stopped playing hockey against us because our team was considered too violent. Even though we would try to restrain ourselves and be nice to other teams so that they would play us, someone in our team would soon lose his cool and destroy our image. An uncle of mine was particularly offensive. He was in his late 40s and no longer so agile, so whenever someone younger passed him my uncle was liable to assault him physically. In the end we had to beg him to give up.

Cricket was a little different. Since there was no physical contact, the aggression came out in the will to win. As a result our small locality produced outstanding sportsmen. My mother's first cousin captained Pakistan in hockey when they won the Olympics. Her brother played both hockey and cricket at national level, and her two sisters' sons captained Pakistan in cricket. Her sister's husband threw the javelin at the Olympics as well as playing cricket for India.

I feel that if somehow the competitiveness of the tribal Pathans could be channelled into sport, they would produce outstanding sportsmen. Not only are they extremely fit and athletic, but they are born with a fighting spirit. I am trying to set up a talent hunt scheme on the periphery of the Tribal Areas so that any exceptional talent can be brought into Pakistan cricket.

The boys I saw playing cricket everywhere since television introduced the game to the Tribal Areas in the early 1980s were exceptionally talented. I was amazed by how well they had picked up batting and bowling techniques simply from watching cricket on television. Wherever in the Tribal Areas there was a reasonably flat piece of land, cricket was being played with anything that resembled a ball or a bat.

PAGES 44-45 *Since the arrival of television, cricket has completely taken over the Tribal Areas. It is played on every sort of terrain, wherever a reasonably flat piece of land is available. Notice the two bemused onlookers of this new game.*

CHAPTER 2

The Southern Tribal Belt

BY FAR THE WILDEST part of the Tribal Areas is Waziristan, the Tribal Areas' southernmost region, from where I started my trip. The terrain is hostile and has played its part in making the inhabitants tough and aggressive. The two principal tribes in the area, the Mahsuds and the Waziris, are both known for their fighting qualities. Most of the time they have fought each other, but they have united against a common enemy. During the British raj these two tribes, along with the Afridis (who live mainly in the Khyber Agency), gave the British more headaches than the whole of the Indian subcontinent put together. Waziristan did not come under British control until the signing of the Durand Treaty in 1893, and during the remaining half-century before Independence the British forces were continuously employed in fighting Waziristan's tribes who refused to accept British dominance. Fifty per cent of the British Indian Army was involved in combatting the uprisings at one stage during the Waziristan Operation, shortly after World War I. No other part of the Tribal Areas witnessed even a fifth of the warfare that went on in Waziristan.

The Mahsuds and Waziris are from the same branch of the Pathan race, the Karlani. The Mahsuds, who comprise two-thirds of the population of South Waziristan, are surrounded by Waziris to the north, south and west. To the east live the Bitanis. Other, smaller tribes found in Waziristan include the Dotani, Sulaiman Khel and my mother's tribe, the Burkis. Waziristan is actually divided into two agencies, North Waziristan and South Waziristan.

The moment we went through Tank and entered South Waziristan, it was like going back in time. As it was early spring, the caravans of the powindahs (nomadic Pathans) were there, on their way back to Zarmelan Plain from the Pakistan lowlands. The scene, with camels, goats and dogs led by good-looking armed men and women in beautifully coloured clothing, was spectacular.

THE MANZAI CANTONMENT

Soon we came to the British-built cantonment (military station) of Manzai, which is occupied by the South Waziristan Scouts. With its outer wall and gun towers, the small cantonment, the site of so much action over the years, conveyed a strong feeling of history. Inside the fortress is a well-planned settlement, which was one of the initial British footholds in Waziristan. There were all sorts of amenities, including squash courts, football grounds, a dairy farm, an ice factory, a hospital and even a ballroom – but a lot of the buildings are now in ruins. Looking around the cantonment, I got a strong sense of hostility from outside. Despite Independence the doors are still closed at night and no one dares step outside. During the days of the British raj, as in most of the Waziristan cantonments, there would be sniping by the tribesmen, often lasting all night. The sniping might not have been effective in terms of casualties, but it served to demonstrate the tribesmen's defiance to the British.

An incident that occurred in Manzai during the British raj gives an insight

PAGE 46 *A Mahsud tribesman. The Mahsuds are the fiercest of all the Pathan tribes.*

PAGE 47 *The bare and hostile terrain of South Waziristan is the wildest part of the Tribal Areas.*

into the macho Pathan character. Apparently the British decided that the cattle stock in Waziristan was not of good quality, as it was yielding neither milk nor meat in sufficient quantities, so a Scottish bull was imported into Manzai to improve the cattle stock. When word got round the area, a jirga (tribal council) was called, the matter was debated at great length and finally it was decided that no British bull would sire local cattle. The next day the British commander of Manzai fort was puzzled to learn that the Scottish bull had been found dead, riddled with bullets.

The Pathan tribe in the Manzai area is the Bitani. On the whole they were allies of the British, because they needed protection from their wilder and more powerful neighbours, the Mahsuds. Many times, however, their suppressed resentment of the British would surface. After all, the British were invaders and, worse still, non-Muslims, while the Bitanis were Pathans with a strong aversion to being ruled. In one instance, in 1860, when the Mahsuds raided Tank, the Bitanis joined in the plundering. Nevertheless, the British expeditionary force could easily subdue the Bitanis, as there was not much cover, and the great technological advantage the British had in arms made it an unequal contest. Also, the Bitanis were a relatively small tribe, and they rarely got help from the Mahsuds.

Shortly before my visit, there had been a mutiny at the Manzai cantonment. The Scouts there had rebelled against an officer who had shot a junior officer he believed had insulted him. In the ensuing rebellion, the officer was attacked by his men and was forced to hide in the officers' mess; two of his attackers were killed. Eventually he was rescued by reinforcements from Tank. When I was there an investigation was going on to find the guilty parties.

INTO THE WILDERNESS

As we travelled into the Sulaiman Mountains, I felt I was entering a wilderness. The last sizeable town before Mahsud country is Jandola, a market town of immense character. We saw all sorts of wild, rugged and handsome characters in the bazaar. Whenever I have passed through the town there has been an interesting mixture of powindahs, Mahsuds and Bitanis, all armed. In 1919 the Mahsuds led by Fazal Din overran Jandola Fort, which was under their control for a while, until the Scouts relieved it.

Beyond Jandola is the land of the Mahsuds. Here the houses are all like fortresses, with high outer walls and gun towers. So rapidly has weaponry technology improved, however, that the gun towers are now obsolete. Today most sub-tribes have rocket launchers and anti-aircraft guns, and nearly everyone possesses a Kalashnikov rifle. I was told that some of the tribes had come

to an understanding that rocket launchers and anti-aircraft guns would not be used in intertribal fighting. This is another example of the Pathans' talent for self-preservation. Recognizing that their warlike nature will sooner or later lead to some sort of conflict but that a no-holds-barred war could cause them immense damage, they accept that it is more expedient to fight within certain rules. Anyone who breaks the rules may incur the wrath of the tribal jirga.

Mahsud villages are scattered all along the road to Wana. The valleys are cultivated, but the terrain is hilly and tough. The reason the Mahsuds are such a tough tribe is very obvious – only the strong could survive in this rugged environment. It must have been hard for any would-be conqueror, as the rocky cliffs offer plenty of protection to snipers. We passed the Shahur Tangi Gorge, where in 1937 a British brigade was ambushed, only a few of the British surviving. One survivor told Colonel Rahamzad Khan, who is the commander of the Scouts at Wana, that the discipline and cunning of the Mahsud lashkar (temporary tribal army) were incredible. Apparently the Mahsuds never broke cover until the entire brigade was within the gorge, then they picked off the drivers of the trucks and armoured cars at the front and rear of the convoy. After that, the convoy was in chaos, and extremely accurate fire from the Mahsuds took a heavy toll. This combination of remarkable discipline and cunning is one of the reasons that the Mahsuds are such a great fighting force, despite being untrained. Their heroics during the 1948 Kashmir campaign were legendary. They not only have an uncanny ability to spot their enemy's weaknesses very quickly, but they also have a considerable amount of patience, which allows them to exploit these weaknesses.

The Mahsuds are without doubt the wildest and fiercest of all the tribal Pathans. The British were forced to send seven expeditions against this tribe alone, yet there was never a long period of peace. In 1860 a British expedition against the Mahsuds was partially successful because the Mahsuds were armed only with stones and ancient matchlocks while the British had vastly superior weapons, especially field guns. Yet the Mahsuds never gave in. They are intelligent and disciplined fighters, but what makes them so deadly is their persistence. When the British started building new posts in Waziristan, after 1860, each British intrusion was met with more Mahsud resistance.

Ultimately, however, it was the Mahsuds' independent nature that

OPPOSITE ABOVE *The more affluent tribesmen have better organized defences, as can be seen in this fortlike house.*

OPPOSITE BELOW *In this rugged area, the valleys are highly sought after for agriculture.*

prevented the British from subduing them. Even the tribal jirga could not stop individuals from conducting a lone war. Near Kanigoram, for example, we were shown a spot where two Mahsud martyrs decided to take on a British brigade in a suicide attack.

The British tried to create a Mahsud Scouts force, but after a few experiments they gave up the venture, as the men were prone to rebellion. They would support tribal uprisings, as was the case in the attack on Wana cantonment by Mullah Powindah, the Waziristan hero who fought the British around the turn of the century; the Mahsud Scouts rebelled and joined the mullah. (Similarly, the Mahsuds in the Baloch regiment during World War I refused to fight against the Turks, who were fellow Muslims.)

It isn't just the British who have suffered at Mahsud hands. The Waziris, who were masters of the Chalweshti plain, eventually had to give it up to the Mahsuds, and they have had to endure a lot of other Mahsud encroachment on their lands. Indeed, the Mahsuds have carried on desultory warfare against the Waziris throughout history. Like the Bitanis, who were forced to ally themselves with the British to protect their lands from the Mahsuds, the Dawar tribe to the north also had to ask for British help. In fact, by playing one tribe off against another, Britain was able to divide and rule – up to a point.

A Mahsud jirga just breaking up in South Waziristan.

Against the North Waziristan tribes, the Mahsuds have rarely fought a losing battle – their fighting genius is legendary. While fighting against the British in 1917, Musa Khan, a Mahsud leader, and six of his fellow tribesmen, dressed as women, managed to enter the Tut Narai post occupied by Scouts and wipe out the whole platoon. In a single year, 1916, the Mahsuds raided Dera Ismail Khan district 17 times. There were two divisions of British troops permanently based at D I Khan just to deal with the Mahsuds. Even before this, under the Sikh protectorate in the first half of the 19th century, the governor of Tank, who was a Tiwana (a member of a Punjabi Muslim land-owning family), was under constant attack from the Mahsuds.

CHANGING PRACTICES

The Mahsuds take the Pathan code of honour, or pukhtunwali (see page 33), to extremes. They truly reflect the independent and democratic nature of Pathan tribal society, where each man considers himself equal to all others.

Like most Pathans, the Mahsuds often hire assassins in cases of revenge. The assassin is regarded as the gun rather than the one who pulls the trigger, and revenge is therefore taken upon the person who hired him rather than upon the assassin himself.

They used to have a particularly violent custom, known as khai, which usually took place between cousins: in a fight one group would kill all the male members of the enemy group and then take over the women. This barbaric custom, which was also practised by the Afridis, has more or less disappeared since Independence in 1947. However, in South Waziristan, a few days after my trip there, and just when everyone felt that the custom of khai had finally died out, all 11 male members of a family were killed by their cousins. Nevertheless, before the killers could take over the property and women of the family whose men had been slain, the tribal jirga intervened and ordered the lashkar (tribal army) to take action. All six adult males in the family that had committed this extreme act of savagery were taken out and shot. I do not think the modern-day tribesman will tolerate khai any more.

In fact, the Mahsuds are not as wild as they once were. One reason is that they are no longer ruled by someone they regard as an enemy. The Pukhtunistan movement (for an independent Pathan homeland) has been dead since the Russian invasion of Afghanistan, and the Mahsuds look upon Pakistan as their own country. The other factor in calming the Mahsuds down is their commercial interests in Tank, Dera Ismail Khan and Karachi. The government has tremendous leverage to confiscate these in instances of Mahsud misconduct in the Tribal Areas. Also, because they now have houses and other

interests in the Settled Areas, they no longer regard these as places to be plundered, as they did during the British raj. The Mahsuds do still encroach on Waziri, Burki and Bitani territory, but on the whole are much more peaceful.

KANIGORAM

The Mahsuds' cultural centre is Kanigoram, the largest town in South Waziristan. This is also the home of the Burki tribe; indeed, the Burkis have always had alliances with the Mahsuds, fighting side by side against the Waziris. Kanigoram is a very historic place, with many old graves.

All the big jirgas (tribal or intertribal councils) used to be held in Kanigoram. The famous Waziristan hero, Mullah Powindah, held his jirgas here. Lashkars would also assemble in Kanigoram. At one time the best weaponry – swords, knives and guns – in Waziristan was made here. Today, weapons are still produced in Kanigoram, but not to the same extent as before. The really big jirgas are things of the past, and there has been no need for huge lashkars since Independence in 1947. Nevertheless, the town remains the Mahsuds' centre.

ABOVE Mahsud girls in South Waziristan.

PAGES 56-57 Kanigoram, the only town in this part of South Waziristan,
is where the Burki tribe is based.

The British first penetrated up to Kanigoram in 1860, their next expeditionary force arriving in 1881. British troops entered the town on several occasions before 1947. They also bombed it, but beforehand would try to let the people know the exact time of the bombing so that they could leave their homes and go into the mountains.

MY MOTHER'S TRIBE

The Burkis in Kanigoram were my hosts, giving me a hero's welcome that was overwhelming. The reason for the great reception was not so much that I was a cricket star but that I was one of their tribe. My mother's branch of the Burki tribe had broken away nearly 350 years ago and settled at Jallandar in India; in memory of them, the Burkis in Kanigoram had named one of the surrounding mountain peaks Jallandar.

The Burki tribe (also known as the Baraki or Urmur tribe) were originally from south-eastern Turkey. In the 11th century they settled in Afghanistan's Logar Valley, near Kabul, after being given land there by Mahmud of Ghazni, the king of what was to become Afghanistan (see page 20). During his invasion of India, Mahmud was particularly pleased with the Burkis' role in the famous battle of Somnath in Gujarat province and, on return, granted them the region now comprising South Waziristan.

It was in the late 16th century that my mother's branch of the Burkis left South Waziristan to settle in Jallandar. They were joined in the early 17th century by Afghan Burkis, who had been deported by the Moghuls after a massacre during an uprising. The Burkis established a dozen fortified villages, known as 'bastis', around the city. They lived in these until Independence in 1947 and were known as the Basti Pathans. One of the earliest bastis was named after the Burki saint Sheikh Darwesh, from whom my grandmother was a direct descendant. His cousin, the famous saint of Waziristan, Sheikh Pir Wali, is buried in Kanigoram.

In South Waziristan, as time went on, the more warlike Mahsuds encroached on the Burkis' territories, and today they are left only with the area immediately around Kanigoram.

Recently the Burkis of Kanigoram had a clash with a Mahsud sub-tribe; we were shown the site of the battle. But, as a rule, the two tribes live on very amicable terms, and the Mahsuds, who outnumber the Burkis by approximately 18 to one, consider them one of their own sub-tribes. In their wars against neighbours, as against the British, the two tribes have fought shoulder to shoulder. The Mahsud children attend Burki schools in Kanigoram, and Burkis and Mahsuds often intermarry.

FIREARMS AND THE OCCASIONAL FEAST

On my arrival in Kanigoram the entire village greeted me with the deafening sounds of Kalashnikov and other rifles – even the odd anti-aircraft gun – fired into the air simultaneously. (This is the Pathan way of welcoming visitors. It can, in fact, be quite scary, as the guns are fired not far above the visitors' heads. When Pakistan won the cricket World Cup there were a few casualties after jubilant Pathans celebrated by firing in the air.)

A lavish feast followed. The feast was served on a cloth, with everyone seated on the ground around it. First the elders ate, then the children and the workers. Nothing is wasted. Tribal Pathans are known for the excellence of their tikkas (mutton or goat grilled on skewers), yet very rarely can they afford to have feasts. Livestock and other food are not abundant in the rugged Waziristan countryside, and a guest doesn't realize how privileged he is to be served goat's meat so lavishly. I loved the roti (a kind of flat bread) – unlike the type served in Pakistan's cities, it is unrefined, retaining all its nutrition. It is not thin like chapatis but quite thick and brown. The other form of bread eaten all over Waziristan is wafer-thin.

The Mahsud staple diet is maize bread, ghee (clarified butter) and yogurt.

Burki tribesmen welcome me to Kanigoram.

58

Meat is a rare luxury. (As a result, the Mahsuds are not big people. They are of medium-height and wiry but extremely agile and strong.) Other food eaten by people living in and around Kanigoram includes a little chicken, spinach, dal (a pulse dish), potatoes, onions, bananas and oranges. Meat, when available, is often cooked in water with no fat added, then the meat is eaten dry and bread is dipped into the broth.

People tend to live to a good age; it is quite common to reach 90. A few of the elders believe, however, that tea – which was introduced into the Tribal Areas by the British – has reduced the life span. It is served everywhere. Green tea is served after meals, but between meals it is made by boiling milk with tea leaves and plenty of sugar. It's delicious and easy to get addicted to – I used to look forward to tea every couple of hours.

The people are extremely fit. Apart from the rigours of life in such a mountainous terrain, with its extremes of weather – from hot to very cold – one way the men keep fit is through dance. As part of their welcome, the younger men of the Burki clan performed a Mahsud dance for me. Apparently derived from

Kanigoram elders show me the site of a recent battle between Burkis and a Mahsud sub-tribe. Despite the occasional skirmish, however, the two tribes coexist quite well, often helping each other against other tribes.

the movements of swordsmen, the dance was obviously meant for fighting men. The movements are very athletic, working all parts of the body, especially the arms and legs. As I watched it, I realized that it performed three functions: strengthening the muscles, improving flexibility and increasing stamina. The dance is to the beat of a drum and can get very fast. Sadly, in recent years, certain members of the clergy have condemned the warlike dance, and its popularity has consequently diminished.

The men's main work is trading and agriculture, but they keep their fighting skills sharp, and, apart from the Mahsud dance, shooting is the principal form of entertainment. I was challenged to shooting competitions all the time, as they knew of my passion for partridge shooting. The standard of shooting is very high – they are excellent marksmen.

In fact, there is still a tradition within certain tribes all over the Tribal Areas whereby the groom is not allowed to take the bride until he shoots and hits a prescribed target. I can imagine the tension some grooms must endure. First they have to go through the nerve-racking experience of finding out what is in store for them as far as their life partner is concerned. (Chances are that, unless she is a cousin, the groom will never even have seen what she looks like – he has to rely on the judgement of the women in his family.) On top of that, he is put on trial to shoot at a coin from about 100 metres in front of a huge crowd before he can take his new wife home!

GENEROSITY AND SELF-RESPECT

The Burkis were unbelievably hospitable, so much so that I was somewhat embarrassed, since I knew that the people's resources were scarce. Certainly it reinforced my belief that generosity has nothing to do with one's material wealth – it is a state of mind.

I was also struck by the respect that the younger members of the tribe accorded their elders. Small boys who had seen me play cricket were courteous, and not once did they make a nuisance of themselves. They were extremely well behaved. I discovered that among the Pathan tribes children become the responsibility of the tribe. If a child misbehaves, he can be disciplined by any older member of the tribe. Throughout the Tribal Areas the

OPPOSITE ABOVE *At Razmak cantonment the Scouts performed a Mahsud dance for us. Similar to the Mahsud dance performed by the Burkis of Kanigoram, it was both warlike and highly athletic.*

OPPOSITE BELOW *Being challenged yet again to a shooting competition, in Kanigoram.*

children are taught to respect their elders, the mothers playing a big part in this. Yet at the same time, the young boys retain their self-respect and don't become meek or submissive.

I remember an incident while I was shooting partridge in the Salt Range in the Punjab. We were walking up partridges on the personal estate of a powerful landlord, and suddenly in front of us we saw a powindah boy of about 13 or 14 years, grazing three camels. The landlord was furious. Not only was the boy trespassing, he was also scaring away the partridges. The landlord sent two of his gunmen to ask the boy to remove himself and his camels from the estate. The men, eager to please their boss, were rude to the boy – who immediately took offence, despite the fact that they were two grown- up, armed men. Both men were momentarily taken aback at the boy's fearlessness. He proceeded to give them a piece of his mind, and then with his pride restored took his camels off the estate.

A teahouse on the way to Makin. Places like this serve food at mealtimes and tea between meals. Camels are parked outside.

A MIXTURE OF OLD AND NEW

Driving from Kanigoram through Mahsud territory, we came to Makin, a historical town that has obviously seen a lot of action. This was where the Mahsuds did their iron smelting, enabling them to produce their weapons. It was ransacked by the British on three occasions, the last time when fighting the faqir of Ippi (see page 66).

At the bazaar at Makin we saw some awesome characters, and the tea stalls in particular gave it the look of the American wild west. We saw a tea stall where camels were parked outside while tough-looking armed men sipped tea around a table. Everywhere there was a wonderful mixture of the old and the new. Datsun pick-ups were parked in the bazaar next to camels. Younger men carried AK47s, while the older tribesmen stuck to their faithful 303s. Clothes were much the same as those worn hundreds of years ago – though, as a result of American aid during the Afghan War, there were a few Pathans wearing

Another teahouse, this one in Makin itself, where we found an incredible mixture of old and new. Ransacked three times during fighting against the British, Makin was the region's main weapon-producing centre.

American GI commando jackets. Most of the tribesmen here, unlike those in more accessible parts of the Tribal Areas, proudly wear their turbans. As in all bazaars in the Tribal Areas, women were not to be seen.

ENTERING WAZIRI TERRITORY

On leaving Makin we entered North Waziristan and Waziri territory. The Waziris are cousins of the Mahsuds. Although they have not been able to match the Mahsuds in fighting capabilities, they are wilder and tougher than most other tribes of the Tribal Areas. Our escort of Scouts had to be on the alert as we passed a village that had had a disagreement with the Political Agent at Razmak. The Scouts were concerned they might try to kidnap us to gain some leverage with him, but in the event there was nothing to worry about. In fact, they had heard that I was coming, and a warm welcome awaited us. We had to decline their invitation for dinner, as we were going on to Razmak.

The building of Razmak cantonment by the British in the early 20th century created a great deal of resentment among the Waziris, and they

In rugged Waziristan everyone has a hard life. These children are taking cover from the extremely cold winds of North Waziristan.

responded by stepping up subversive activities against the British. Until Independence in 1947 the outer doors of the huge cantonment walls would be closed at sunset, when the sniping used to start. They lived in a continual state of siege. Pakistan's present Finance Minister, Mr Sartaj Aziz, whose father was posted as an officer at Razmak Fort, told me how all government officials and British troops could move out of the fort only in a protected convoy. They knew they would be the targets of sniping, so there was always a sense of danger and adventure. Sometimes there were only a few snipers, but the Pathans regarded it as a matter of principle – they had constantly to demonstrate their defiance. On one occasion Mr Aziz's father was watching a football match by the fort when suddenly sniping started and someone was killed.

The cantonment was segregated, with the British and native quarters in different parts; predictably, the British quarters were far superior. At Independence the entire Razmak cantonment was ransacked by the tribesmen after the British vacated it. It was some years before it was reclaimed by the Scouts. I was put up at the governor's house, one of the most impressive colonial

At Razmak cantonment we stayed in the governor's house, a splendid legacy of the British raj.

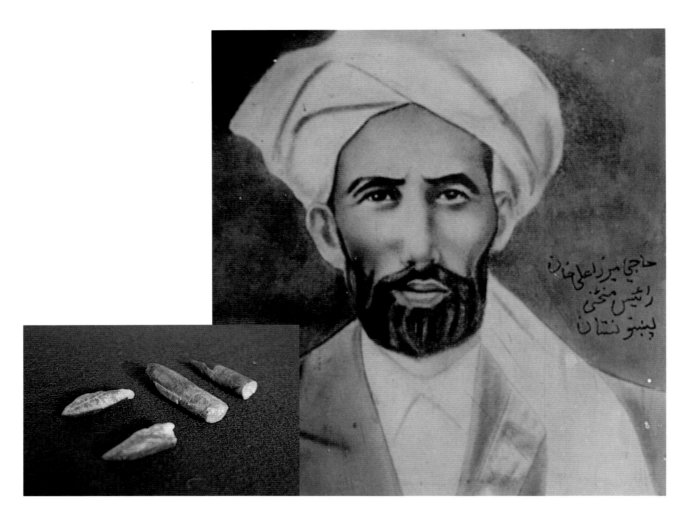

حاجی میرزا علی خان
رئیس منځنی
ﭘﺸﺘﻮﻧﺴﺘﺎﻥ

buildings in Waziristan. It was very comfortable – despite the cold nights and the high ceilings and huge rooms, the wood fire kept the room warm.

A public school has recently been built at Razmak, and children from all over the Tribal Areas come here to board. My old school teacher, Major Langland (an Englishman), became the first principal of the school. One day he was bemused to find that gunmen had entered his house. They made him leave with them at gunpoint, and later he found out he had been kidnapped because he had refused admission to the son of one malik while admitting another malik's son. He was released after the Political Agent intervened.

.

THE FAQIR OF IPPI

At Razmak I was introduced to Malik Noor Baqi Jan. He was a malik of the Tori Khel Waziris, who were known to be among the best fighters of the Waziri sub-tribes. Always a problem for the British, they had helped the 20th-

MAIN PICTURE *The faqir of Ippi was a Pathan hero who fought the British in the decade leading up to Independence in 1947.*

INSET *The faqir was credited with supernatural powers. At the officers' mess in Miranshah, we saw the pebbles he had turned into bullets.*

century Pathan hero, the faqir of Ippi, throughout his struggle. Malik Noor Baqi had met the faqir (a faqir is a poor man or one who has given up worldly goods), who had fought the British from the mid 1930s till Independence in 1947 and never been defeated. Malik Noor Baqi was one of his greatest admirers, and he told me that the faqir was a slight man but was extremely fit, very intelligent and completely fearless. It was said that he had supernatural powers, that Allah helped him whenever he was in trouble. He could predict where the British were going to attack and would vanish long before they could reach him. He could turn pebbles into bullets – we saw some of them at the officers' mess in Miranshah. In one battle, near Razmak, the faqir and 32 of his followers repulsed an attack by an entire brigade; it is said that the British never believed they were fighting just 32 men.

The faqir's rise to prominence began when a Pathan schoolteacher, Noor Ali Shah, fell in love and married a Hindu girl, Ram Kori, in Bannu. As the girl had not reached the age of consent, the British justice demanded that the girl be returned to her parents. Once the court decided that the girl was not legally married to the young Pathan, the parents took the girl and left Bannu for the Punjab. It is said that they married her to a fellow Hindu in Hoshiarpur. Noor Ali Shah meanwhile was married to a cousin. After a year of restlessness he finally left his wife and child to go to India in search of his love – never to be seen again. Following the court's decision, a young mullah (a Muslim priest) sprang into prominence when he gave a fiery speech at this injustice according to Islamic law. That was the first time the British heard of the faqir of Ippi.

From 1935 the faqir waged guerrilla war against the British. In 1936 at Majka in the Khaisora in North Waziristan, 2300 British and Indian soldiers were killed; the weather helped the faqir, as the British force suffered heavy losses in the rain, hail and floods. In 1937 at Damdel a British force was ambushed by the faqir, inflicting heavy casualties. Although he got no support from Afghanistan's King Zahir Shah (who feared that the British might remove him from the throne), the Pathan tribes of North Waziristan supported him in one way or another. The faqir had drawn so much attention to the Noor Ali Shah incident that Bitanis, Marwats, Khattaks, Dawars and Waziris all backed him against the British. Some volunteers from Pathan tribes in Afghanistan joined the faqir in 1936, even though the Afghan government discouraged it.

By keeping on the move, the faqir managed to evade the British. They tried conciliation and, at the same time, intimidation, bombing the faqir's hide-outs at Arsalkot. They also tried to bribe members of the clergy to speak against the faqir. There was, for example, a faqir of Shiwa who was persuaded to do so – but nothing could stop the whole of North Waziristan being on fire from 1937

to 1947, when Pakistan gained its independence, by which time 40,000 British troops were involved in fighting the faqir of Ippi. In 1940 Hitler sent two German advisors, who improved the faqir's gun-making and helped in guerrilla training. Four big guns were made in the faqir's armoury. After 1947 the faqir became a spokesman for the Pukhtunistan movement for an independent Pathan homeland, and was shunned by Pakistan.

Malik Noor Baqi had served as a Khassadar during the days of the British raj. (Because Khassadars were armed men provided by the tribes and paid by the British to protect the Political Agent, any attack on the agent would involve attacking the Khassadars too, setting off a blood feud; they thus served as a useful deterrent. The system is still in use today.) Malik Noor Baqi's sympathies, however, were always with the faqir of Ippi – as, indeed, were those of all the Khassadars, Scouts and Pathan soldiers in the Indian army. The Khassadars would apparently inform the faqir of any British plans against him. There were even cases of Scouts being court-martialled for deliberately not shooting straight at the faqir or at members of their own tribes. Just before Partition, Malik Noor Baqi was instructed by Ayub Khan – then a Brigadier but later to

These houses in the Tochi Valley in North Waziristan always remind me of medieval castles.

68

become President of Pakistan (from 1958 to 1968) – to tell the faqir that he would leave ammunition for him at a certain place. With such widespread support, it is no wonder that the faqir was a substantial thorn in Britain's side.

SERVING THE ENEMY

Malik Noor Baqi told me how he himself used to join the other tribesmen at night and snipe away at the British – whom he served during the day. According to him, the Pathans hated the British (though they had hated the Sikhs even more): Britain was seen as an enemy who was trying to take away the Pathans' independence. He told me how from time to time, between the 1920s and Independence in 1947, villagers were bombed by the British without any warning, and many women and children died along with the men. Most of the time leaflets were dropped beforehand to warn the villagers to seek the safety of the mountains, but apparently the leaflets were occasionally either dropped on the wrong spot or not dropped at all. Malik Noor Baqi also

Malik Noor Baqi Jan, shown here (wearing the turban) next to me, served as a Khassadar during the British raj, when he had known the faqir of Ippi. Next to him is fellow cricketer Zakir Khan, a Pathan who accompanied me on this trip.

spoke of the many sacrifices the villagers were prepared to make during the British blockades just to preserve their honour and independence. Sometimes during the blockade they survived in the hills on nothing but acorns.

Nevertheless, the Pathans did respect two traits in the British: their administrative skills and their bravery. The British officers who served on the north-west frontier were exceptional men. In the first place, only those with a sense of adventure volunteered to serve here. But they were also forced to be brave, because the Scouts were enlisted from the tribesmen, and their British officers were aware that any act of cowardice meant that they stood to lose the respect of their men – men whose main criteria for judging a man were based on his courage. Some British Political Agents actually got very close to the tribesmen, and a few even identified with the tribes.

The Scout force was built up by the British in an attempt to deal with guerrillas such as the faqir of Ippi. By enlisting the Scouts from the tribes and

This large jirga held in North Waziristan has just finished meeting. They were trying to resolve a dispute between two Waziri sub-tribes over the proposed construction of a dam.

giving them army training and superior weapons, it was hoped that they would find it much easier to deal with the rebellious Pathan tribes than the regular army did. The British were usually very careful to post the Scouts outside their own tribe's territory, however, so that their fierce tribal loyalty would not get in the way of executing their duties.

MALIK NOOR BAQI'S LIFE

Malik Noor Baqi inherited the position of malik from his father. It means regular income, something that everyone in the Tribal Areas wants desperately, since life there is so uncertain and insecure. He has a house in Miranshah as well as one in his village near Razmak. He prefers to spend the summer in the wonderful Razmak climate; it rains every afternoon for two hours, and for the rest of the time there is beautiful sunshine.

Maliq Noor Baqi has 22 children: 12 from his first wife, and 10 from his second wife, whom he married when the first wife refused to have any more

A market in North Waziristan.

71

children. He told me that when the second wife also decided against further children, he had contemplated marrying for a third time – but finally decided he had enough offspring. In the Tribal Areas the strength of a man depends upon the number of sons he has, though only the rich and powerful can afford the luxury of a second or third marriage. Malik Noor Baqi wanted his sons to spend as much time as possible in the Tribal Areas, as he felt they would get physically much hardier than if they grew up in the Plains. He refused to let his daughters study, as he thought it would be wasted – instead, he married most of them off to influential young men.

As we moved further into North Waziristan from Razmak, we passed a war zone. There was a conflict between two Waziri sub-tribes: the Asad Khel were fighting the Durdani over the proposed construction of Serobi Dam. We also saw a huge jirga trying to resolve the conflict.

THE MADDA KHEL WAZIRIS

One of the most interesting villages I visited in North Waziristan is that of the Madda Khel Waziris. It really does look a wild place. Like the Mahsuds, the Madda Khel Waziris did not allow any Afghan refugees in their area. From the village to the Afghan border, cars are not allowed into the Madda Khel territory. There were lots of camels in the village when we were there, and we soon found out why the village is literally the end of the road. Apparently, 45 years ago, 260 of the tribal elders had taken a vow that in order to preserve their independence, no schools or roads would enter the Madda Khel heartland. As a result camels have remained the only form of transport.

A friend of mine, Ajmal Khan, who is a federal minister and a member of the Pakistan National Assembly, comes from this area. When Ajmal's father died a year ago, he took his body in a jeep to his village for burial. The tribal jirga was incensed that their law had been broken, even though he was carrying the body of his father. They fined him two Kalashnikov rifles and one pistol – and this despite the fact that he was a minister of Pakistan.

The younger tribesmen find this oath of the tribal elders regressive. I discussed the matter with Wadood Khan, who was the son of a tribal malik, Nasrullah Khan. He said that his generation was waiting for those elders who had taken the oath to die so that they could build roads and schools and bring electricity to the area. He felt that if they wished, they probably could change it, but it was out of respect for the tribal elders that they were not doing so.

The staple diet here is dal roti (lentils and bread), and the men looked extremely fit. However, much of the Mahsud and Waziri resources are spent on buying arms, and it is usually at the expense of agriculture. The money that

should be reinvested in agriculture is used instead in preparations for blood vendettas. In purely economic terms, blood vendettas retard progress. Near the village we saw a disputed area, where a few days previously 18 men had been killed in a gunfight. While the tribal jirga was in the process of taking a decision about it, both factions were arming themselves to the teeth.

FORGIVING AN ENEMY

Even so, blood feuds do sometimes end in forgiveness. I was told of one such case by a Waziri tribesman named Haji Bahram Khan. According to him, a Waziri tribesman, who had gone to Mecca for the Hajj (the sacred pilgrimage), decided on his return that he could not pursue a blood vendetta against a particular sub-tribe any longer. (This man, incidentally, had been mainly

ABOVE *A village in Madda Khel territory beyond which cars cannot go, because 40 years ago the tribal elders vowed not to allow schools or roads into their land.*

PAGES 74-75 *This North Waziristan village, the heartland of the Madda Khel Waziris, was one of the wildest places I visited. A few days before I arrived 18 men had been killed in a gunfight over some disputed land, and more bloodshed was in the offing.*

responsible for some 40 deaths in that sub-tribe over the previous 20 years.) He therefore dressed as a woman, with his head covered, and walked into the house of his enemies. Once in, he told them that he had been to Mecca and that now they should either kill him or forgive him, and the blood feud should end there. Apparently, the women persuaded their men to forgive him, saying that it would be cowardly to kill a man once he had walked within the four walls of their house.

A MAHSUD FRIEND

On my second visit to Waziristan I was accompanied by a friend, a Mahsud tribesman who works for the Pakistani government. I had got to know Dost Mohammad when he was working for the government in Gilgit, in the Northern Areas. Initially he struck me as rather ill-suited to being a civil servant, lacking both the subservience and the discipline such a post often requires. In fact, I discovered that he had had quite a few skirmishes with his superiors, and the only reason he had not been kicked out of the civil service was his charming nature, sharp mind and great sense of humour which make it impossible to dislike him.

Dost Mohammad had volunteered to come with me to Waziristan's Mahsud country in order to show me some true Mahsud hospitality. I hadn't realized how much fun I would have as a result. He gave me a running commentary on the Mahsud way of life, based on his conviction that his own tribe is superior to all the others. This is a common trait among Pathans, who at times may actually refuse to acknowledge other tribes as even being Pathans at all. Their loyalty is first to their home, then to their sub-tribe, next to their tribe and finally to the whole Pathan race.

Although I am not from the Mahsud tribe, Dost Mohammad began to follow cricket because of his pride in the fact that a Pathan had captained his country in cricket. Like most tribesmen he has strong views on everything – there is no question of sitting on the fence. For example, he feels no compunction about the Mahsuds' having encroached upon Burki, Waziri and Bitani lands. To him the matter is clear-cut: the Mahsuds are the best fighters, and in the Tribal Areas it has always been acknowledged that might is right as far as intertribal relations are concerned. This is no place for the weak to live; they can always go to the Settled Areas. Like all Pathans, he is most impressed by bravery. He is very proud of his five-year-old son because at school he is known to take on two or three boys at a time in fights.

OPPOSITE *Waziri tribesmen of North Waziristan.*

Dost Mohammad was full of heroic stories about how his father and grandfather fought the British, despite not having the arms and equipment to
compete with them. He also told me how his father fought in Kashmir in 1948
to liberate it from Indian rule. Indeed, the Mahsuds fought brilliantly in Kashmir. Three hundred Mahsud tribesmen captured the hills surrounding
Srinagar. They held their positions for two days but had to withdraw in the
end, as there were no supplies of food or ammunition, and the Indian Para-
troop Regiment had landed at the airport.

While we were travelling towards Wana, we came across a caravan of powindahs, the nomadic pathans. Looking at a powindah woman, Dost Mohammad
was reminded of an incident that occurred a few years ago. A beautiful powindah woman came to his house in Waziristan to sell some clothes, and while she
was displaying the clothes, she caught Dost Mohammad eyeing her rather
lecherously. Suddenly the saleswoman was transformed. In absolute fury she
told him that her husband was an extremely powerful man and that if Dost
Mohammad ever saw him he would die of fright. She then added that she
could herself snap him in two just with her legs. He was highly embarrassed

*An Afghan Mujahideen refugee village in North Waziristan. During
the Afghan War over three million refugees crossed the border to live in
refugee villages in Pakistan.*

by all this, as it took place in front of his wife and mother. Since that day Dost Mohammad has been careful to keep a healthy distance between him and the powindah women.

In fact, Dost Mohammad has strong views about women. He is completely devoted to his mother, treating her with the greatest respect and love. He told me about how his wife was selected for him without his ever having set eyes on her. After their wedding she lived in their house for almost a year before he was allowed to consummate his marriage. I had not heard of this before, but apparently it often occurs in the Tribal Areas when a young bride is not considered old enough to fulfil her responsibilities as a wife. There is no hard-and-fast rule as to what age is old enough, as it depends on the maturity of the girl, but among the Mahsuds, girls generally marry between the ages of about 14 and 18.

According to Dost Mohammad, the wearing of a lot of make-up is often frowned upon in the Tribal Areas. Women are preferred with their natural beauty. He quoted an instance where two sisters who had gone to have a look at a possible bride for their brother were sent back by the prospective bride's mother because they were wearing too much make-up. Dost Mohammad also told me how he himself, when travelling with his wife to a wedding in Islamabad, had been annoyed when she put on some lipstick. He made her take it off, as he felt she should only make herself attractive for him and that there was no need for her to look good in front of other people. This was despite the fact that, marriage ceremonies being segregated, she would have been in the women's section.

Dost Mohammad's attitude is typical of the Pathans' possessiveness towards their females. Yet he is an educated man who, despite the conservative side to his character, is extremely progressive. He is having his daughters educated, even though there is very little education of women in the Tribal Areas.

He believes that there is no reason why the tribal people should not be educated, now that the British are no longer ruling India, though he suspects that there are some maliks who are against this because their own powers would diminish. He has little respect for the maliks, as he feels they were a creation of the British who used them in an attempt to control the Tribal Areas. (Before the arrival of the British, maliks were respected members of the tribe, like elders, but the British introduced the system of paying them allowances.) Dost Mohammad feels that even now they are not performing any useful function and are more interested in their own well-being than that of the tribe.

He is critical of the Maliki system (see page 27), feeling it is out-of-date and breeds corruption. He advocates adult franchise in the Tribal Areas so that the

people can decide their own fate. Like all Pathans, he hates the FCR system (see page 28), in which, if a crime is committed in the Tribal Areas by one Mahsud, for example, all members of his sub-tribe in the Settled Areas can be apprehended by the government just on the orders of the Political Agent.

Dost Mohammad despises the tribesmen who worked for the British as soldiers, either as Scouts or as Khassadars and, he feels, sold their souls. He is puzzled by certain civil servant colleagues who are remnants of the British raj: having replaced the British, they have adopted their habits and characteristics, and speak English to their children. He is contemptuous of Pakistanis who try to become English and are embarrassed about their own culture.

Like most Pathans, Dost Mohammad has no idea how old he is. I discovered this when I asked him what star-sign he was. He replied that all he had been told was that he was born a few years before his father left for the Kashmir jihad (holy war) in 1948. To a Pathan, age is measured not by years but events.

ABOVE *This was taken during the month of fasting, when we were weak with hunger, and I had fallen asleep. The man in uniform is Colonel Rahamzad Khan, commander of the Scouts at Wana. Next to him (in the white shirt) is my friend Dost Mohammad, a Mahsud tribesman who accompanied me on this trip. On the far left is fellow cricketer Zakir Khan.*

OPPOSITE *A Mahsud tribesman. Only the strong survive.*

CHAPTER 3

The Central & Northern Tribal Belts

NORTH OF WAZIRISTAN is Kurram Agency, which takes in the fertile valley of the Kurram River. After travelling through the wilderness of Waziristan, I found the green Kurram Valley, with its terraced rice paddies and fruit orchards, a glorious contrast. Because of clashes between the Shia and Sunni Muslims in the Kurram Agency, carrying arms is illegal, so the area is tame compared with Waziristan, and we generally found the atmosphere relaxed. As we drove up the Kurram Valley towards the town of Parachinar, we noticed that not all the houses were built like fortresses, as they are in Waziristan. There were some which had verandas and which were relatively accessible. The higher we went, the more beautiful the valley became. On the right the snow-covered peak of Safed Koh ('White Mountain') towered over us. At Parachinar the valley widens considerably. Here I stayed in the Governor's house, another elegant colonial building. It has been well preserved, whereas many other colonial relics in the Tribal Areas and the rest of Pakistan have been replaced by inferior modern structures.

AFTERMATH OF THE AFGHAN WAR

The border with Afghanistan is only a couple of hours' drive from Parachinar, and we saw here the devastation resulting from the 1979 Soviet invasion of Afghanistan and the subsequent war. Driving up to the Trimangle Pass, which is at an altitude of more than 2400 metres, we saw a village at the base of the pass that had been hit by rockets fired by the pro-Soviet Afghan government. At the top of the pass, there was a destroyed Afghan post. The whole area was controlled by the forces of the Mujahideen guerrilla commander, Gulbuddin Hekmatyar. We saw his camp, carefully camouflaged in thick pine forests. This was just about the only area that was still covered by trees. All around, massive deforestation had taken place. The Afghan refugees, who had no source of income, became involved in the timber trade to make ends meet. As a result, we saw everywhere barren hillsides and the consequent soil erosion.

We crossed the Durand Line into Afghanistan, as there are no Afghan government checkpoints or posts at the border – the government's presence is restricted to the cities, and everywhere else is controlled by the Mujahideen. Across the border we saw a village that had been completely destroyed by Soviet helicopter gunships. The turning point of the Afghan War was when the Mujahideen acquired Stinger missiles, which put an end to the effectiveness of the helicopter gunships. The Mujahideen we met believed that if the United States had supplied them with Stinger missiles earlier, there would not have been such prolonged bloodshed. They felt that the missiles had not been supplied earlier because the United States wanted to bleed the Soviets rather than go for a quick victory. When I was there the Mujahideen victory over the

OPPOSITE *Feasting at the top of Trimangle Pass, on the Afghan border, with soldiers of the Pakistan army who are based there. Pir Yacub Shah, a Burki from Kanigoram who is a malik and the Political Agent of Kurram, is on my right.*

PAGE 82 *A shepherd boy from the Kurram Valley.*

PAGE 83 *In the Kurram Valley the houses became less like fortresses, reflecting the prolonged periods of peace and security the area has enjoyed.*

pro-Soviet Najib government was imminent, and there was a general sense of optimism among the guerrillas, who were weary after years of fighting. A few months after my visit, the Najib government fell to the Mujahideen.

While we were at the Trimangle Pass, I came across a couple of Afghan boys who were carrying small Russian mines. (A lot of border areas were mined by the Russians.) The boys told us they were taking the mines to the Tribal Areas to sell. Apparently they had devised ways of defusing the mines by themselves and would actually look for mines to defuse and then sell. A number of boys were involved in this, most of whom had known no other life except war. A boy now in his teens would have been only around five or so when the Russians invaded, and for him war is a part of life. Indeed, we met some Mujahideen who were barely out of their teens and were complaining that they were bored, because since the Russians had left there hadn't been any real action. They were thinking of joining the jihad in Kashmir.

WAR AND PEACE IN THE VALLEY

The Kurram Valley is inhabited mainly by Turi Pathans, who are Shia Muslims, and by Bangash Pathans, who are Sunni Muslims. Like most Pathans, the Turis were originally semi-nomadic, spending winter by the Indus and summer in the Kurram Valley. The Turis are said to have abandoned this semi-nomadic lifestyle about three centuries ago after an incident involving some of their women. The story goes that the women were teased by some Bangash tribesmen, and the outrage so incensed the Turis that they went to war with the Bangash, driving them out of the Kurram Valley and settling there themselves. Subsequently, however, there were constant encroachments on their land, both from the west and especially from the Orakzais to the east, so the Turis occupied the areas they could defend.

In the mid 19th century (before the Durand Line was created to separate Afghanistan and India), the Afghan government made the Kurram Valley its domain. Shortly after, the first British expedition entered the valley, to put an end to raids made into the British-ruled Kohat district from the Kurram Valley. After the second Afghan War, in 1878, the valley became independent of Afghan rule, and complete anarchy prevailed. The Turis, worried about the constant Sunni attacks, petitioned the British for help, who were happy to oblige, since they needed Kurram as a base for launching an invasion of Afghanistan. In 1892 the British annexed the Kurram Valley and began to pay annual allowances to the tribe. In return, the Turis paid land revenue to the British and served in the British Indian Army and in the Scouts.

There was relative peace and quiet in the Kurram Valley till 1919, when, in

the third Afghan War, an enterprising Afghan general, Nadir Khan, swept up the Kurram Valley as far as Thal, where his troops besieged the fort. The Waziris of the nearby Tochi Valley, on the North Waziristan border, rose up against the British at this time too. After the war, the Kurram Valley was again occupied by the British until Independence. Ever since then, the valley has been fairly calm, apart from the occasional Shia-Sunni skirmish.

As a result of the Soviet invasion of Afghanistan and the recent war, the Kurram Valley was flooded with Afghan refugees, who at one time numbered over 350,000. Following the Mujahideen victory, a small number of refugees have now begun returning to Afghanistan.

A SETTLED WAY OF LIFE

Unlike Waziristan, Kurram is a rice-eating belt. Rice is grown on the terraced hillsides, and both the Bangash and the Turis have rice in their meals once a day. They look more like Pathans from the Settled Areas, having had a relatively secure life as a result of the British presence. Nevertheless, they still live according to the Pathan code of honour. Hospitality, revenge and honour are

ABOVE *This village in Afghanistan, near the border, was destroyed by Soviet helicopter gunships.*

PAGES 88-89 *Wheat and rice are the principal crops in the fertile Kurram Valley.*

still prominent in their value system. Although they might not practise pukhtunwali with the same ferocity as the Mahsuds and Waziris, or adhere to the code quite so strictly, all life is conducted along the same principles.

SAMANA FORT

From the Kurram Valley we went on to the Samana fort, which is at an altitude of about 2000 metres. The fort overlooks the Hangu Valley to the south; to the north are the mountains of Tirah. From here we could also see the Gunahgara Plain at the foot of the mountains. This was where Ahadad Khan led the Afridis to their great victory over the Moghul army (see pages 22-23). The Afridi tribe's summer heartland, in the upper Tirah, is due north-west of the fort, but as there is no road, it is a five- to seven-day journey by foot.

Built by the British in about 1910, the fort was also used as a summer resort by the Political Agent during the British raj. Samana has excellent weather in the summer, when it is sunny but cool, with occasional monsoon rains. In the winter there are snowfalls and it gets quite cold.

We spent a night in a rest house next to the fort. The house had been built since Independence – during the days of the British, all the houses were built

A Turi village in the Kurram Valley.

within the fort. It is an attractive spot but a little too populated for my liking. There are houses everywhere, and every possible piece of flat land is cultivated. Even land that is not flat has been terraced and planted with crops. The population explosion here is fairly recent – about 25 years ago the area was well forested and there was plenty of wildlife to be found. Sadly, this is the story of most of Pakistan, where the rapid population growth has put tremendous pressure on the land. Deforestation has been a direct result, with devastating consequences for the dams (because of soil erosion) and for wildlife.

THE ORAKZAI TIRAH

To the south-east of the Kurram Valley is Orakzai Agency. It covers the southern part of the Tirah Mountains, an area known as the lower Tirah or Orakzai Tirah, since it is inhabited by the Orakzai tribe. Because I didn't know anyone from this tribe I had to enlist the help of the Political Agent to visit the region. Though extremely helpful, he was reluctant to let me go. He feared that members of the Orakzai tribe might kidnap me to embarrass the administration and to obtain concessions for the tribe. Seeing my resolve, however, he sent the Assistant Political Agent and an armed escort with me.

It was early spring when we visited the lower Tirah, just after the rainy season, and all around us was fresh and green. I found it one of the most beautiful landscapes in the whole of the Tribal Areas. We travelled from Hangu towards Kohat and after 16 kilometres turned into the mountains along a river valley.

As we went higher up the valley the fortifications of the homes became formidable. Just before we reached Kalaya, which is the heartland of the Orakzai Tirah, the houses began to resemble medieval European castles. Indeed, were it not for the electricity cables, a visitor might think he was somewhere in medieval Europe – except that the fortlike houses are made of mud. One of the reasons that the people prefer mud exteriors throughout the Tribal Areas is that mud resists bullets better than brick or cement does. The other reason is that mud walls keep the interiors warm in the winter and cool in the summer, unlike cement, which does the opposite.

At Kalaya the valley widens. When we were there, it was completely green after the spring rainfall. The weather was perfect – cool, sunny and fresh during the day and cold at night. There were a variety of wild flowers growing all over the place, and wheat was grown on every available piece of flat land. The livestock looked healthier than those I had seen in Waziristan; indeed, cows, goats and sheep are generally much larger in the northern tribal belt than they are in Waziristan.

A large percentage of the inhabitants of the valley around Kalaya are Shia

Muslims. We saw a lot of the Orakzai Shia women going to an Imam Bara (Shia mosque) for a funeral. The women here wear black all the time. On the north-eastern side of the valley we crossed a bridge and suddenly found ourselves in the Sunni Muslim area. Here the women dress as in the rest of the Tribal Areas (where the Sunnis are in the majority), in bright-coloured clothes, especially red.

The Orakzai share their territory with Pathans originally from other tribes. Known as hamsayas, meaning 'neighbours', these tribesmen are considered part of the Orakzai tribe for all practical purposes.

There is a Scouts' post in Kalaya but it was built after Independence. The Orakzai allowed it to be built because the Pakistani government set up a school and a small dispensary in the area.

ABOVE *Girls fascinated by the camera in the Orakzai Tirah.*

OPPOSITE *A river valley in the Orakzai Tirah.*

A WORLD APART

The Afridi tribe inhabits the northern Tirah Mountains, known as the upper Tirah or Afridi Tirah, which is part of Khyber Agency, and as we approached the border between the Orakzai Tirah and the Afridi Tirah, we had to leave the road and continue on a mule track. At this point the Assistant Political Agent accompanying me became a little agitated. I could see he was particularly concerned as we approached a village guarding the valley leading to upper Tirah, but despite his protests we drove into the village.

Here there was no electricity. As at Kalaya, all the men were armed, but somehow they looked more ferocious. When we told them the purpose of our visit, however, they became extremely hospitable. Immediately, tea was ordered, but before they could start to cut up a goat or chicken to cook for a feast, we stopped them, insisting we could not stay long. Somehow I was never at all frightened in the Tribal Areas. Wherever the tribesmen had heard of me, I was treated as if I belonged to their tribe; they took great pride in the fact that I was a Pathan. And wherever they had not heard of cricket or of me, as was the case in this village, they were still warm and friendly once they

This house is built on a natural fortification (raised ground) in the Orakzai Tirah, a landscape which contrasts dramatically with Waziristan.

94

knew the purpose of my visit. The only problem I had was when I had to turn down their hospitality, which at times almost annoyed them, as though I felt it was not good enough for me.

I would have gone on into the upper Tirah, but the Assistant Political Agent was adamant that he could not take any more risks. He insisted that if anything happened to me, his job would be on the line, so I reluctantly turned back. In any case, going to upper Tirah would have meant a four-day trek as there were no roads. Also, because of the rainy season, crossing the streams, in which the water level was very high, would have been a problem.

We came back along the valley of the Barra River. Wild and beautiful and almost uninhabited, the valley was green and covered by undergrowth, but coniferous trees could be seen only in the high, inaccessible areas. Water from the Barra River is supposed to be better than any other drinking water. The people who live in the area, as well as the population of Peshawar, which also gets water from this river, swear by it. Apart from containing minerals that keep the people exceptionally healthy, it is said to be extremely good for the

On the border of the Orakzai Tirah and the Afridi Tirah, and approached by mule track, this was the last village I was able to visit in the Tirah. The inhabitants, all of whom were armed, looked fierce but were actually very friendly and hospitable.

95

digestion. We ate a huge feast of mutton kebabs – my favourite being skewered liver with fat wrapped round it – and after a couple of glasses of Barra water I was ready for another feast.

KHYBER AGENCY

Khyber Agency, which is inhabited by Afridis, takes in the Khyber Pass as well as upper Tirah. The rugged and hostile terrain of the Khyber Pass reminded me of Waziristan. But because of the pass's importance as the main route from Pakistan to Afghanistan, and indeed the gateway to the subcontinent, the people there are used to outsiders. They are not as wild as the tribesmen of either Waziristan or upper Tirah, who are more cut off from the outside world.

Nevertheless, for the past 400 years the Afridis have been a formidable tribe, fighting the Moghuls, Sikhs and British with great ferocity. They were hard to subdue due to their inaccessible Tirah highlands and their toughness, bred into them through having to survive in a challenging climate and terrain.

It is common to find Afridis with blue or green eyes. Like most tribal Pathans, the Afridis are semi-nomadic. They spend summer in Upper Barra and Maidan (in the upper Tirah) and move to Bazaar and Khajuri in the winter because the upper Tirah is too cold then. The more affluent Afridi families move to Peshawar in the winter.

In the upper Tirah the Afridis live with hamsayas ('neighbours'). Hamsayas are members of a weaker group affiliated to a tribe, and here they are mainly Hindus and Sikhs. No intermarriages take place between the Sikhs, Hindus and Pathans, and the hamsayas are slightly subordinate, but they are nevertheless given tribal protection and tribal rights and privileges. Until the turn of the century, the Hindus were obliged to wear trousers that had vertical red stripes, so they could be distinguished from the Pathans, and so they could be protected. Basically traders, the hamsayas were originally brought in to do jobs that Pathans did not want to do themselves. Often musicians were imported, because although the Pathans loved music, it was not macho to become a musician. This practice existed elsewhere in the Tribal Areas too; the 'Basti Pathans' (Burkis who lived in Jallandar), for example, had non-Pathan musicians, and it remains the custom in the Tribal Areas to this day.

OPPOSITE ABOVE *Weapons in the Tribal Areas are highly sophisticated and up-to-date. A rocket launcher is among the weaponry of these young armed Afridis in the Khyber Pass.*

OPPOSITE BELOW *Sikhs and Pathans coexist in the Tirah. No intermarriages take place, but they live in complete harmony.*

The Afridis moved into upper Tirah and Khyber in the 16th century. Ever since they have controlled the Khyber Pass. Until Independence they considered it their right to exact a toll from anyone seeking access (though this is no longer the case, since they do not regard the Pakistan government as alien).

The Moghuls, who ruled the subcontinent from the early 16th to the late 18th century, clashed with the Afridis a number of times, suffering heavy defeats at Katakushta and again on the Gunahgara Plain (see pages 22 and 23). In the 19th century their successors, the Sikhs, also clashed with the Afridis; in the Peshawar region, one of the Sikh ruler Ranjit Singh's generals, the Italian Avitable, paid a bounty for every Afridi head brought in by Pathan landlords.

The initial British advance into Afridi territory was in 1839, during the first Afghan War, when along with a Sikh force they entered the Khyber. Before then, the Pathans harboured no prejudice against Christians. In 1809 Lord

ABOVE *Feasting with Afridis at a village in the Khyber Pass. (My cousin, Sohail Khan, is seated at the right.) The Afridis considered it their right to exact a toll from anyone travelling through the pass.*

OPPOSITE ABOVE *With Scouts in the Khyber Pass.*

OPPOSITE BELOW *The famous Khyber Pass. The railway and road were major British achievements.*

Elphinstone, who was leading a British diplomatic mission to Kabul, had marked the British arrival in the North-West Frontier by a picnic on top of the Kohat Pass with the Bosti Khel Afridis. And Alexander Burnes, another British agent travelling to Kabul, remembered that even in the 1830s, when he passed Jalabad, he was allowed to sleep in a mosque, despite being a Christian. There was a high degree of religious tolerance. But once the British had become the masters of the Punjab in the early 1840s, they had to deal directly with the Afridis, which brought them into confrontation. Hence in the next half-century the British had to send a number of expeditions to subdue them.

In 1896 the British launched the Tirah campaign against the Afridis and the Orakzai, who joined forces to resist them. 60,000 men, under General Lockhart, were sent in during the biggest operation ever undertaken in the region. Setting up headquarters in Maidan, they sent punitive expeditions in all directions, destroying vital fruit trees and walnut trees and burning villages. Yet, although this operation subdued the two tribes temporarily, it achieved little. The Pathans, though badly outnumbered and outgunned, used guerrilla tactics to force the British to retreat back to Peshawar, and within a few years the Afridis and Orakzais had resumed their customary raids into British India. Never again did the British venture into Tirah.

DIVIDE AND RULE

The British were forced to use all their skills in diplomacy, as well as their genius for manipulation, in their dealings with the Afridis. They realized that the best way to prevent the tribes from concentrating their energies on fighting the British was to keep them in conflict with each other. This divide-and-rule policy was quite easy to practise among a race that had so many intra-tribe and inter-tribe rivalries. For example, the British would pay allowances to either the Adam Khel Afridis, the Bangash or the Orakzai for them to keep the Kohat Pass open, then if one of the other two tribes committed an offence, the tribe receiving payment would declare war on them. In the Khyber Pass the British were less successful, however, as the Kuki Khel Afridis could not be bribed.

During the third Afghan War the Orakzai wanted to help the Afghan king but were prevented from doing so by the British, who bribed a mullah to instigate a Shia-Sunni quarrel in the Tirah. In the ensuing conflict between the Sunni Afridis and the Shia Orakzai, more fruit trees were destroyed and quite a few young men died. The British also bribed some mullahs to start a campaign of maligning the dynamic king of Afghanistan, Amanullah: the mullahs claimed that the king's modernization plans were un-Islamic. (The British did

not want a progressive and modern Muslim government in Afghanistan which they could not control. Moreover a strong Afghanistan would have serious implications for the Indian Muslims and the Pathan tribes.)

THE GUNSHOPS OF DARRA ADAM KHEL

Enterprising businessmen, the Afridis set up their own gun factories in the town of Darra Adam Khel, situated in the narrowest part of the Kohat Pass. The town began making imitations of British guns in the 19th century. Although the replicas were good, their biggest problem was manufacturing bolts, so they would invent ingenious ways of stealing bolts from the British soldiers. For over a century Darra Adam Khel has been completely given over to the manufacture of guns and ammunition. Gunshops, with workshops behind, line the main street and back alleys. Replicas of weaponry from all over the world are manufactured by these family businesses. The skills are passed on from father to son, and children become skilled craftsmen.

A gunshop at Darra Adam Khel, a town that is entirely given over to weaponry production.

One of the ultimate humiliations of a tribal Pathan is to have his gun snatched: a man would rather die than have his gun forcibly taken by his enemies. My Mahsud friend, Dost Mohammad, told me how three armed men had once tried to snatch his rifle. He was only a schoolboy at the time and was petrified. However, he decided that he would prefer death to humiliation, and the men, seeing his resolve, were impressed by his courage and left him alone.

MOHMAND AGENCY

Mohmand Agency is north of Khyber and is the home of the Mohmand and Safi tribes (in the southern and northern halves respectively). There are also a few Utman Khels on the eastern border. The countryside is very bleak. I found the dry, treeless plains and barren hills a sharp contrast with the green

ABOVE *An Afridi malik talking to me near Warsak Dam in Mohmand. It was here that Alexander the Great started his trip along the Kabul River, eventually travelling down the Indus to the Arabian Sea.*

OPPOSITE *In 1897 Winston Churchill, then war correspondent for the London Daily Telegraph, covered an uprising just east of Mohmand Agency from this observation post, where he nearly lost his life. Known as Churchill's Picket, it has panoramic views of the Swat Valley. In the foreground are Buddhist ruins dating from over 2000 years ago.*

valleys and mountains of many other parts of the northern tribal belt, such as Kurram, the Orakzai Tirah and, to the north of Mohmand, Bajaur Agency. The unproductive land has resulted in large-scale migrations into the Peshawar Valley to the east, and many Mohmands are now found farming in the Settled Areas.

An incident that occurred while I was visiting Mohmand brought out an interesting Pathan characteristic. We were on our way to photograph a picket used by Winston Churchill when he was a war correspondent at the turn of the century. There was an armed escort in front of us and another one behind.

As we overtook a jeep, our driver was not concentrating and he accidentally hit the jeep on the side. It was only a slight bump and no one thought much of it as we drove on. The driver of the jeep, however, caught up with us and gestured for us to stop – which we did. A Mohmand tribesmen aged about 50 jumped out, looking absolutely livid. He addressed our driver in Pashtu, asking for an explanation. I was amazed at this, as our driver happened to be a rank holder in the Scouts, was very tall and built of solid muscle, and was a tribal Pathan himself. On top of that our driver was armed, while the Mohmand tribesman was not. Moreover, on this occasion there were six armed Scouts in front of us and another six in the van behind us.

Despite this great discrepancy in the strength of the two parties, I was astonished to see our driver apologizing profusely and looking extremely sheepish. Satisfied that he had extracted an apology, the Mohmand got back into his jeep and drove off. If a tribal Pathan knows that he is in the wrong, he is as meek and cowed as a sheep – but if he believes he is in the right and feels he has been unjustly treated, he is like a wounded tiger.

We went to the most attractive part of Mohmand, the area around the Warsak Dam on the Kabul River. It was here that Alexander, in 320 BC, started travelling down and charting the Kabul River and then the mighty Indus.

BAJAUR: THE NORTHERNMOST AGENCY

Bajaur Agency, the northernmost of the agencies in the Tribal Areas, is the home of the Tarkalani and Utmankhel tribes. I went there after Pakistan had won the cricket World Cup in 1992. The reception I was given was wild even by Kanigoram standards. The moment word went round, the youth of Bajaur mobilized any form of transport they could get their hands on and came after me. It was nice to receive such an enthusiastic welcome, though it disrupted our tour and, especially, photography.

OPPOSITE *A crowd welcoming us in Bajaur.*

Like most of the northern tribal belt, the Bajaur Agency is green. It has rich agricultural land and produces enough wheat to feed the whole area. The people we saw were not always armed, and there was a generally peaceful atmosphere. This was mainly because the Tarkalani tribe, the inhabitants of the northern half of the agency, are tenants of two major landlords, or khans, who own most of the land.

In many ways this part of Bajaur could almost be considered feudal – indeed, the khans had absolute feudal power over their subjects until 1974, when the government took over these powers, leaving the khans their property rights and status as chiefs. Yet the individual farmer has enormous self-respect. Even though the landlords are powerful, they have to be careful how they treat their tenants. (This is in marked contrast to other parts of Pakistan. For example, in Sind province the people have suffered at the hands of the higher classes, and in both Sind and Punjab provinces the people at the bottom of the feudal hierarchy are servile and downtrodden.)

The southern half of the agency is the home of the Utmankhel tribe. Being part of the Karlani branch of Pathans (see pages 18-20), they are, true to character, more democratic. They have neither the khans with all their trappings of power and influence, nor the feudal structure found among the Tarkalanis. Instead, they have a large number of maliks, who can only lead and influence the sub-tribes if their policies are perceived to be good for the tribe.

I went up to Nawa Pass, which is on the border with Afghanistan. This was the pass through which Alexander entered India more than 2000 years ago. The first of the Moghuls, Babur, followed the same route into India in the 16th century, describing in his autobiography how he went on to spend a few weeks in the Bajaur Valley enjoying its climate and fruits. (The British too invaded the Bajaur Valley in 1897, after crossing over the Malakand Pass, in a vain attempt to subdue a large-scale Pathan rebellion.)

The Scouts' post on the Nawa Pass looks down into Afghanistan. We were treated to goat tikkas (kebabs) and grilled chicken. I really enjoyed the food in the Tribal Areas. Contrary to the modern trend, I love meat, and I've never tasted better meat than the mutton and goat they grill on skewers. They also grill pieces of fat taken from the tail of the sheep – something that I have not seen anywhere else in the world. It is absolutely delicious.

OPPOSITE ABOVE *A house resembling a medieval castle in the middle of the fertile Bajaur Valley.*

OPPOSITE BELOW *A Scouts' fort, a legacy of the British raj, in the Bajaur Valley.*

We were driving down from Nawa Pass when we were stopped by a Toyota pickup overflowing with young boys wanting to congratulate me on Pakistan's World Cup triumph. I was highly impressed by the boys, who despite their immense enthusiasm shook hands and took autographs in an extremely disciplined manner. There was no pushing, no shouting, none of the rude questions I've had elsewhere, outside the Tribal Areas, such as when was I planning to get married. One 13-year-old boy particularly impressed me. We shook hands and then he proudly handed me a five-rupee note for my cancer hospital appeal, declaring that he was giving according to his means. I was very touched, the more so because, though he realized it was a small amount, he was not embarrassed about it, as it was all he could afford.

THE TRAGEDY OF MAMOONA
In Bajaur I was told of the famous tragedy of a local girl. Mamoona was a young girl of incredible beauty, and everyone in the Bajaur Valley knew of her beauty. She was married to Sher Alam, a proud and handsome man from her tribe. Once when he was away, a stranger knocked at their house. When

At Nawa Pass, on the border between Bajaur and Afghanistan, we were treated to delicious goat tikkas.

Mamoona opened the door, the man asked whether he could borrow some tobacco. She obliged him with some and he left. When Sher Alam returned he was told that his wife had given tobacco to a stranger. He was furious. Mamoona apologized, saying that she had not realized there was anything wrong in it.

For two days Sher Alam was on the horns of a dilemma. Knowing that the village was aware of the incident, he felt humiliated that his wife had opened the door to a stranger. At the same time he loved her immensely and couldn't even think of replacing her. After two days he made up his mind: he could not live with the shame, and so he killed Mamoona.

The moment word went round, the villagers were so incensed that they drove Sher Alam out of the Bajaur Valley. I asked why they had not killed him, and they replied, what greater punishment was there than for him to live his life without the beautiful Mamoona? Also, some members of the tribe in a way sympathized with him, since he had killed her for honourable reasons and must have died a thousand deaths before he could bring himself to kill her.

Being greeted by enthusiastic youths in Bajaur. They were ecstatic about our World Cup triumph.

CHAPTER 4

The Powindahs

FOR ME, BY FAR the most fascinating people in the Tribal Areas are the powindahs, the nomadic Pathan tribes that for centuries used to come down to India in the winter and move back to Afghanistan in the summer. Every year between 200,000 and 500,000 powindahs would move into the Tribal Areas from Afghanistan through the Gomal Pass. They used to come down in military formation because they were constantly attacked by Mahsud and occasionally Waziri tribesmen as they passed through the Tribal Areas and into the Derajat plains. During the British raj they were given protection by the Scouts (the soldiers enlisted from the tribes and specially trained to

deal with the Tribal Areas) and in return were expected to help the British by informing or fighting against the Mahsuds. Since Independence, however, there have been few instances of Mahsud harassment. In fact, there have been intermarriages and alliances between Mahsud and certain powindah tribes.

In 1961 the powindahs were stopped from entering Pakistan because of the Pukhtunistan movement (for a Pathan homeland). It was felt that Afghanistan was sending subversive elements with the nomads. They went through extreme suffering as a result, many facing starvation. In addition, much of the NWFP was devastated because of its dependence on the powindahs' trade. After that a lot of powindahs were settled in northern Afghanistan by the Afghan government. During the 1979 Russian invasion of Afghanistan, General Zia allowed powindahs to come into Pakistan, but they were refugees. Currently, the powindahs move only from South Waziristan to Punjab and Sind for the winter and then back to the South Waziristan highlands for the

ABOVE *Powindahs passing through the Shahur Tangi Gorge on their way back from the plains of Punjab in April.*

PAGE 110 *Tractor-trolleys are replacing camels as the form of transport of many of the more enterprising powindahs.*

PAGE 111 *A powindah encampment in South Waziristan. The powindahs live in perfect harmony with their animals.*

summer, and their numbers have diminished, especially since the Afghan War. A small percentage, however, have kept their traditional routes despite the war, travelling from Ghazni in Afghanistan to the plains of Pakistan.

The other Pathans tend to look down upon them because the powindahs have to rely upon others when obtaining permission to pass through their land. To a Pathan, being at someone else's mercy is a failing – they value their independence above all. I believe, however, that the powindahs are the most adventurous and enterprising of all the Pathan tribes. At one time they were traders, bringing products from Afghanistan and Central Asia to be sold in Indian markets. Before the creation of Pakistan, they used to cross right over to Calcutta. In the spring they would head back to their homes in Afghanistan and South Waziristan with products from India to sell.

Trade is no longer the major reason for their movement, as improved communications have made this form of trade redundant. Now their migration is basically for survival. They need to find new pastures for their animals and employment for themselves in the Settled Areas. The complex irrigation

ABOVE *A powindah encampment, near Wana; here they have to rely on the Waziris for safe conduct.*

PAGES 114-115 *Powindahs stopped near Manzai, a resting place for them for hundreds of years before proceeding to the Sulaiman Mountains.*

113

system of Punjab and Sind owes a lot to the powindahs, who were responsible for digging some of the canals as well as cleaning up many of them. The powindahs are extremely industrious and are prepared to work for very little money. For them, jobs in cities are easy compared with the rigours of their tough nomadic life. They are also known for their honesty.

The only flaw in the powindah character from the Islamic point of view is that through the centuries they have practised money-lending. In Islam, lending money at an exorbitant rate of interest is not allowed, as it has destroyed so many families over the centuries. Apart from money-lending, in all other respects the powindahs are strict Muslims.

PATHAN KINGDOMS

The incredible thing about the powindahs is that they were the only Pathans to set up kingdoms in the Indian subcontinent. For two centuries, India was ruled by the Khaljis, Lodhis and Suris – Pathan dynasties that belonged to the powindah tribes. The last Pathan sultan was overthrown in 1526 by Babur, who established the Moghul empire (see page 21). But even after the Pathan empire in Delhi had fallen into the hands of the Moghuls, another powindah tribe, the Nuharnis, ruled Bihar and Bengal for almost 100 years.

Sign of the times: the tractor-trolley. Camels are still used too, however.

The Lodhis and Suris are sister tribes of my father's tribe, the Niazis. The Golden Age of the Niazi tribe was under Sher Shah Suri. Arguably the greatest Pathan king, he deposed the Moghul emperor Humayun, the son of Babur. Sher Shah Suri ruled India from 1539 until his death in 1545. One of his leading generals, Haibat Khan Niazi, who was the governor of Punjab, was my ancestor. After Sher Shah Suri's death he made a bid for the throne, but was defeated and killed. The Niazis have not held any power since. Today, most of them live in the Isa Khel and Mianwali districts on either side of the Indus River. There are also Niazi settlements in Baluchistan and in Ghazni in Afghanistan, and there are still Niazi powindahs who come down from Zarmelan in South Waziristan every year. Since the Afghan war, however, many of them have settled in Dera Ismail Khan district.

AN EARLY FRIENDSHIP

It was the fact that nomads could actually make themselves rulers of most of the Indian subcontinent that made me so interested in the powindahs. My interest was awakened not just by their glorious past, however – I have actually been fascinated by them ever since I was a small boy. When I was seven, my parents took pity on a powindah boy who had come to Lahore to sell some goods. Though 15 years old, Ahmad could barely speak Urdu (the official language of Pakistan) and he had no idea of how to sell anything. My parents decided to give him shelter when they discovered that he had had hardly anything to eat for days. Gradually they found out why he had broken away from the rest of his tribe. Apparently, Ahmad had shot his cousin after a quarrel. Realizing that he now faced death, he had run away. My parents decided that he could stay in our home, and he became a part of our family.

I liked Ahmad because he was a good shot with my air gun. One incident, however, has always remained in my mind. Ahmad had shot a dove, which fell into our neighbour's garden. When Ahmad went to collect the bird, the owner of the house came out. Seeing a wild boy in his garden, he shouted at him to get out, and at the same time swore at him. To a tribal Pathan, being sworn at becomes a matter of honour. Ahmad retreated from the garden and sulked for a while. Then he set his jaw and got up as if he had finally made up his mind.

I was extremely excited when he made his intentions clear to me. He was going to kill the man. 'How?' I asked. He told me he would break into the man's house when he was asleep and then stab him. 'How will you know where he is sleeping?' I persisted, unable to contain my sense of drama and adventure. He replied that he was going to make a reconnaissance trip to the house in the evening.

Here it is important to explain how a Pathan's mind functions when he is out to seek revenge. Not only must he preserve his honour but he also has to think of his family's welfare in case he is killed. The tribal Pathan will therefore very rarely make a foolish attack. Ahmad did not try to kill the man immediately, as he might have been tempted to do, for his mind was working in another way. He probably suspected that in a frontal attack the older and perhaps stronger man might injure him; or the man could possibly get a gun from the house, or call his servants. At night, on the other hand, Ahmad could take him off guard, and then escape before anyone knew what happened.

I was so excited by all this that I could not keep it from my mother. She immediately squashed his plans through emotional blackmail, saying that the police would put her in prison. That did the trick, because it would have been awful for Ahmad if his hostess, and someone he felt indebted to, suffered as a result of his action. Nevertheless, Ahmad was as hostile as ever to the neighbour. Eventually my mother, who was in constant fear that Ahmad might do something silly, persuaded the man to apologize to him.

After a year, Ahmad went back to his home, and we thought that we would never see him again. It was obvious his nomadic blood made him too restless

A powindah encampment at sunrise.

to stay in one place. Yet a couple of years later he returned, bringing a lot of gifts for us, including a powindah dog, which was the best present he could ever have given us. Apparently the cousin he had shot had survived, and Ahmad had been forgiven and accepted back.

ZARMELAN PLAIN

The Pathan race divides into four great branches (see page 18), and the powindahs are of Ghilzai stock. As well as the Niazis, Lodhis, Suris and Khaljis already mentioned, other powindah tribes include the Nasir, Dotani and Sulaiman Khel. The stronghold of the Sulaiman Khel, the largest of the powindah tribes, is the breathtaking Zarmelan Plain. It is a historic place because, apart from the powindahs' annual migration, many conquerors came this way, crossing the Gomal Pass then camping at Zarmelan before going on to the plains of India. Mahmud of Ghazni, the king of what was to become Afghanistan, camped with his army in this vast plain a thousand years ago.

There is something strangely beautiful about Zarmelan, with its miles and miles of flat land surrounded by hostile mountains. Apart from the occasional powindah encampment, it is completely untouched. The Pakistan

Zarmelan Plain. 'Zarmelan' means 'a thousand miles', an appropriate name for this vast and beautiful wilderness.

119

government, however, is trying to develop the area, so that it can become the bread basket for the whole of Waziristan. Tube wells are being sunk, fruit trees planted and some land brought under cultivation. I felt a little sad that such a magnificent wilderness will be tamed, but I suppose it will make life much easier for this wild race.

DIGNITY AND POVERTY

Life is extremely tough for the nomadic tribes. I met a powindah with his family while they were on their way back to Zarmelan from Dera Ismail Khan. He had not eaten for two days. His wife looked as if she too had sacrificed her food so that the children could eat. When I asked him whether he would like to settle down, he replied that he would give anything to have a little land where he could build his home and feed his animals. I then asked him why he did not accept some employment in the Settled Areas. His reply was that he could never live in someone's house or quarters and be dependent on them for his and his family's livelihood – he would rather die.

Not surprisingly, the most frequently uttered prayer of every Pathan is, 'God, don't make me dependent on anyone.' To retain their independence and self-respect, the powindahs lead the hardest possible life. They never have enough money to buy land and build their own homes, so they have to keep moving to wherever they can trade or find pastures to feed their animals. Yet never once did I see a powindah begging. Despite their poverty they have not lost their pride and dignity, and that for me is their greatest quality.

Through the centuries the powindahs have travelled all over northern India to subsist; only those who had lucky breaks were able to settle down. That is why they have been the most enterprising of the Pathan tribes – so much so that they set up their own kingdoms. The British recognized this attribute, taking powindahs and their camels to open up the West Australian Desert in the late 19th century. I have met the descendants of the powindah families in Perth, in Western Australia.

LEGENDARY VALOUR

When the powindahs were prevented from crossing over to Pakistan from Afghanistan in 1961, many tried to jump the government blockade. The Scouts' mess in Wana told me some incredible stories of valour relating to the Sulaiman Khel tribesmen. In one shoot-out between 12 Sulaiman Khel guns and a platoon of Scouts, the Sulaiman Khel guns were silenced only after a long battle. The Scouts then discovered that two tribesmen had been wounded and the rest killed. They could not believe that only 12 men had put up such a fight against such odds. The only reason the wounded had stopped firing was that they were out of ammunition. These two men were taken to hospital, where they refused to be anaesthetized before the operation. They simply put their turbans between their teeth while the bullets were removed and they were stitched up. Once the operation was over, they wanted to get up and leave immediately. Most people would stay in hospital for months after sustaining such wounds.

The commander of Scouts at Wana, Colonel Rahamzad Khan, told me of an instance where he had gone to condole with a Sulaiman Khel malik whose young son had died fighting the Russians. The malik was in pain that his handsome young son had been cut down in the prime of his life. But when the colonel tried to commiserate with him, the malik proudly said that there was nothing to be sad about, as his son had died fighting like a man not a coward.

On another occasion, while we were driving in the wilderness of the Zarme-lan plain, we saw a middle-aged woman carrying a heavy load on her head. When we stopped and asked if we could help her, she first came and shook hands with us and then politely declined, explaining that she had to go where our jeep would not be able to. The colonel asked her whether she was frightened to be by herself in such a wild place. In reply she took out a huge Waziri knife and said that anyone who came close to her would have to deal with that.

THE POWINDAH WOMEN

The powindahs are the only Pathan tribes in which the women go unveiled, even when they go to the Settled Areas or areas outside their villages; they wear beautiful, long, highly colourful dresses. Whenever they see alien men, they simply turn their faces away. Like all Pathan women, they refuse to have their photographs taken.

One of my great-uncles married a powindah girl. In his and my father's village, Mianwali, the powindahs until about 1960 would leave their womenfolk with various families, while the men went off to trade and make money in the cities. The powindah women would work in the houses and be treated as part of the family. There was never any question of any type of sexual harassment towards them, despite their great beauty. In the spring the men would return and take their women back.

It is interesting how various duties are divided among the men, women and children when they are on the road. The men get the camels ready, while the women look after the tents, cook, clean and get firewood. The children help to

PAGES 122-123 *Powindah women in discussion near their tractor-trolley.*

get the firewood and take care of the baby goats, and the whole family looks after the other animals.

For me the best time to observe the powindahs is just before sunset, when they have set up their tents and are preparing for the night. An incredible air of harmony exists between the men, women, children, dogs, goats, camels and, occasionally, cows. I have seen similar scenes of harmony between humans and their animals in villages at sunset in the Karakoram Mountains, but somehow the sight of the powindahs always affects me in a deeper way. It is something quite unique. Their days are so tough, especially when they are on the move and every member of the family has to work. Sunset is the time when all the work is done and the whole family relaxes together with the animals. It always touched me to see how people leading such a hard life could find time every day for so much happiness together.

ABOVE *Seated in front of her tent, an elderly powindah woman looks upon her son and grandchildren. The powindahs have exceptionally close-knit families.*

OPPOSITE ABOVE *Women at an encampment in South Waziristan.*

OPPOSITE BELOW *Training in looking after the animals is begun early in powindah families.*

CHAPTER 5

The Pathan Women

THE PATHAN WOMEN living in the Tribal Areas are strong and beautiful. Sadly, the beauty does not last long, due to their extremely tough lives. The powindah women, for example, not only cook, clean and fetch water and wood, but they also manage the camels if necessary. The powindah women's babies are delivered as the tribe travels, and often the caravans do not even stop long enough to give the women time to recuperate. Throughout the Tribal Areas a woman is the pride of the family. No man will ever tolerate an insult to his mother, wife, sister or daughter. A family's honour depends on its womenfolk being protected, and a man will go to great lengths to protect them. According to the tribal Pathans, God made women physically weaker and much more vulnerable, and consequently in need of men's protection.

In most parts of the Tribal Areas, women are relatively free to move about in their own villages, though they cannot trade or go to the bazaar. On the rare occasions that one meets a woman in the Tribal Areas, she shakes hands. Outside of their own villages, however, women are much more restricted. A woman will not accompany her husband, brothers or father to any place where she is likely to come into contact with alien men, for the family knows that if the woman is harassed or molested in any way, the men will have no option but to avenge the insult at the risk of their lives. If they were to back away from such an action, for example in a situation in which they were faced with greater odds, then they would fail in the eyes not only of their fellow tribesmen but also of the woman herself. In fact, it is the women who insist on strictly imposing the pukhtunwali code (see page 33) and their Islamic values.

When tribal Pathans visit a city, therefore, their women will avoid going with them, preferring to stay with their families, in the knowledge that they will have complete protection and security. For Pathans the city is an alien place, where there are no tribal laws or tribal values to protect women.

When Pathans go to live in the Settled Areas and especially the cities there, such as Peshawar, Tank or Dera Ismail Khan, the women can literally be imprisoned within the four walls of the house. Some Afridi women who were interviewed on my behalf said how much they preferred living in the Tirah highlands to Peshawar for this reason.

On one occasion I met a Sulaiman Khel tribesman who had settled in Lahore as a trader. After establishing their trade, he and his brother had arranged for their wives and children to join them. When the men went to

OPPOSITE *An old woman in Waziristan. Women look older than their years in the Tribal Areas because of the hard life they lead. But age is associated with wisdom, and so elderly women are treated with great respect. The home is their domain.*

PAGE 126 *The tribal way of avoiding strangers who have a camera.*

PAGE 127 *Women working in the fields in the northern tribal belt. Although they do not go to public places like the bazaar, they are free to go outside the home in most parts of the Tribal Areas.*

PAGES 130-131 *Women fetching water in North Waziristan. Carrying water from the river is just one of the arduous chores that make women's lives very tough.*

work, they would lock the door, leaving their wives and children inside the house. To an outsider this might look as though the women were being enslaved, but in reality they all felt that it was the only way to protect the women in alien surroundings and an alien culture.

OBSERVING PURDAH

If women do ever accompany their men to the city, they will be in complete purdah (covered from head to foot). Indeed, purdah is very strictly observed the moment women go out of their villages. By this custom, a family indicates to everyone that the women are decent and should be treated accordingly.

Purdah means that a woman has to dress and behave in such a way that she does not provoke or tempt the opposite sex – in other words, she must behave and dress modestly. The purdah system is based on the belief that the clothes a woman wears determine how she is treated by men, and that if she wants respect, she should dress according to what her society considers respectable.

What purdah actually entails varies considerably from area to area. In Waziristan a woman will simply cover her head with a shawl-like garment known as a chador; whenever she passes by a man, she just looks the other way. By contrast, in a few other places, such as Thal, at the edge of the Kurram Valley, a woman will wear a burqa, in which she is completely veiled from head to foot. The burqa is, however, rare in most parts of the Tribal Areas. It is much more common among the Pathan women living in the towns of the Settled Areas of the NWFP, where they have less freedom.

In Kanigoram the Burki women have always been more conservative than the Mahsud women from the surrounding areas. Perhaps this is because Kanigoram is the only town in the area, or it may be that the Burkis are fundamentally conservative.

SEGREGATION AND SECURITY

Pathan women have always observed purdah when going to the cities, but over the past 15 years or so, with the worldwide renaissance of Islam, the segregation between men and women has increased in the Tribal Areas. In Waziristan, for example, the Mahsuds told me that there had been less segregation previously. At one time, among the Mahsuds and various other tribes of Waziristan, the women would even embrace men they knew when greeting them. Also,

OPPOSITE *A typical market scene, in which women are completely absent. Women avoid public places where they are likely to come into contact with men.*

the Mahsud dance, now performed only by men, was danced by men and women together. Since the 1970s, however, the dancing together of men and women has been discouraged, and it now occurs only between cousins at wedding celebrations in some villages throughout the Tribal Areas.

The Pathans of the Tribal Areas view segregation of the sexes as essential not only to avoid any temptation but also because they feel that men and women were meant to perform different functions on earth. They do not see a conflict between them – the two are supposed to complement each other.

As a result of this highly defined code of behaviour, women have immense security. They know that, provided they observe purdah, no man will dare harass them. During blood feuds and tribal warfare, women are spared. It is considered cowardly for the victor to dishonour the womenfolk of the vanquished, and there have been instances where the victor has provided food to the wife and children of a slain enemy.

There has been no known rape case in the entire history of the Tribal Areas.

ABOVE *Young girls already being trained to wear chadors but still uninhibited about meeting alien men.*

OPPOSITE *Girls are taught at an early age to dress modestly.*

(The other reason for the absence of rape and for the relative freedom women have in their own villages in the Tribal Areas is that everyone knows everyone else in their particular area, and identifying the culprit would be extremely easy. Yet in villages elsewhere in Pakistan, for example in Punjab and Sind, despite everyone knowing everyone else there are rape cases – usually initiated by the socially powerful against the weak.)

The Pathans have in fact taken Islam to extremes. In Islam itself women have enjoyed considerable freedom. A woman must dress so that she does not provoke men, but this should not limit her activities. The Prophet gave permission for a woman to lead the prayers in a mosque. His first wife was a businesswoman, and his second wife was considered by many to be an authority on Islamic customs. She also led a faction in the civil war following the Prophet's death. Islam gives women equal dignity to men; before being married, for example, a woman has to give her consent, and she has the right to refuse an offer. Sadly, at times in the Tribal Areas she is not given the choice. Nevertheless, the Tribal Areas do follow Islam in according the mother a higher status than the father in a family.

PILLARS OF STRENGTH

A woman is the sole power in the Pathan household. She takes major decisions within the home, and she makes the children respect their father. Above all, she ensures that the Pathan code of honour is upheld by her family, because that is the criterion by which her children will be judged in society. In the famous case of Ajab Khan's kidnapping of Molly Ellis (see page 26), Ajab's wife insisted that he must avenge the dishonour the British had brought on Ajab's house.

The Pathan mothers continually recount stories of valour to their children. As the Pathan poet Ghani Khan says, they tell their children that a coward dies but his screams last forever. There is a Pushtu song in which a mother tells her son, who is going to battle, that she would much rather he died a brave man than lived as a coward. It reminds me of the last Moorish king of Spain, Abu Abdullah, who, as he was leaving Granada after having been ousted by the Catholics, looked back at what had been his kingdom and began to weep. His mother, on seeing this, admonished him, 'Stop crying like a woman over what you could not defend like a man.'

If a woman's husband is killed, she will make sure that her sons avenge his death; if a son is too young, then she will prepare him for the time when he is old enough. There was a tragic case where a Mahsud woman, whose husband died fighting the British in the late '20s, vowed to avenge his death. Refusing

to remarry, she prepared her son from childhood to avenge his father's death. Suddenly one day, in 1947, she heard that the British were leaving, so she told her son that he must act soon, otherwise he would have to go to England for revenge. The son went to Tank and shot the British Political Agent. The tragic irony was that the Political Agent, Duncan, was an Englishman who greatly admired Pathans and even sympathized with their cause.

Pathan women always discourage self-pity in children. I will never forget when, as a boy of 10 or 11 years, I was listening to the radio, which was playing a love song about a man who was suffering because his loved one had left him. At this point my mother's sister walked in. When she heard the male singer complaining about how cruel his beloved and the world were for making him suffer, she contemptuously dismissed the man, saying that he was pathetic and that only a weak man would behave like a woman. In other words, strong men were not supposed to have such emotions. This attitude is very characteristic of Pathan women, who dismiss any form of weakness in their males because they come from environments where the weak would find it hard to survive.

(What actually constitutes weakness can be surprising. When we were at Wana cantonment, my companion, Zakir Khan, had an upset stomach after yet

The clothing of the powindah women is particularly colourful and striking.

another feast. When Dost Mohammad was told, he was disgusted and told Zakir to keep quiet about the fact so that no one should find out. He felt that if someone discovered we were travelling with a man who had such a weak constitution, it would be embarrassing for all of us. Even an upset stomach is a sign of weakness to a Pathan – man or woman.)

All household work is done by women, including fetching firewood and water. This can be exceedingly tough in the mountainous regions of the Tribal Areas, and it takes a heavy toll on the women, who rapidly begin to look older than their years. While the women are working, the men look after the children, trade, shop and keep themselves fit for fighting.

The women are strong, both physically and mentally. While we were driving in the Zarmelan Plain, I witnessed an incident that stuck in my mind. A tribesman, with his wife, baby and son of about four years, stopped our escort, which was in front of us. It was the middle of nowhere, and obviously there was a problem with one of the children, which forced the man to ask for a lift. The driver must have asked him to jump in the back of the van, where there were four soldiers seated.

The man got into the high Toyota van first, and the driver, thinking they were all in, started to move off, just as the woman, who was carrying the baby, tried to get in the van. We feared that she might fall, injuring herself and the

Fetching water in Waziristan. At times this can involve walking quite a distance, so women have to be physically strong.

138

baby, but we need not have worried. Like an Olympic pole-vaulter, she gracefully scaled the tailgate with the support of her free hand. Her son, however, was still not in as the van was beginning to pull away. Just as we were about to panic she athletically swooped down and with one arm picked up the boy as though he were a plastic doll. Astonished, we watched this superb display of suppleness, strength and athleticism. Her chador had slipped during these movements, and we saw that she was a stunning beauty, barely 20 years of age. Interestingly, not once did the soldiers sitting opposite even look at her; this was a mark of respect for both the woman and her husband.

During wars, the women carry food and ammunition to the men. Most can handle a gun and have been known to fight alongside their men in times of need. In the 16th century, when my ancestor, Haibat Khan Niazi (see pages 117 and 143) was betrayed by the Kashmiris during his rebellion against the sultan, Islam Shah, he was surprised and attacked by an overwhelming force. His small band of Niazis fought valiantly to the end, and Haibat Khan's wife fought with great valour alongside her husband. She died with him, the sword still in her hand. Among the Basti Pathans in Jallandar (see page 55), there were instances where the women helped the men to defend their bastis (fortified settlements) from Sikh attacks.

There was a case recently in Barak, in the Khyber Agency, involving an Afridi woman who was married to a man her two brothers didn't like. One day the brothers decided to ambush her husband. She happened to spot them laying the ambush, and shot both of them dead. Afterwards, she told her father that if they had hated her husband so much, they should not have allowed her to marry him in the first place, but that now she was married, she had to protect her husband. The aggrieved father saw her point and let the case rest.

In another recent incident in the Khyber Agency the Afridi women staged a demonstration protesting against the imprisonment of their men under the FCR system (see page 28).

Like the men, the tribal women cannot be pushed around, no matter how poor their background.

NO PLACE FOR ILLICIT ROMANCE

The Tribal Areas are not the place for Romeos and Juliets. The only marriages that are sanctioned are the arranged marriages. A couple which elopes knows the score: if caught, they both face death. No one in the tribe will give the couple any protection. Their only chance is to seek refuge in another tribe, preferably one that is hostile to theirs. Apart from incurring the wrath of the girl's family, elopement is also discouraged by the tribal ethics. Indeed, the tribe will actually assist in finding the couple, who can never feel entirely safe, even if they make it to the Settled Areas.

A few days before I arrived in the Orakzai Tirah, a Shia girl had eloped with a Sunni boy. The Shia tribe was up in arms, and unless the boy and girl were handed over they were prepared to go to war. Even though the couple was married, the girl was returned to her family and shot. The boy escaped into the Afridi Tirah.

Several years ago my second cousin and neighbour, Ansar Khan Burki, shot dead a distant relative, who had encouraged Ansar Khan's niece to leave her husband so that he could marry her instead. Ansar Khan shot the man during my niece's wedding in Zaman Park, and he was in such a frenzied state that he ended up shooting the man's uncle too. He is now facing a death sentence.

If a man finds out that his wife has been unfaithful, he will kill her first and then approach the tribal jirga to demand either that they hand over her lover for him to shoot or that they execute the man. There is no question of the lover receiving any protection from his family or friends; in fact, a father will even hand over his son for execution.

However, although all this may sound as though it is an everyday occurrence, in fact it serves as a deterrent; in any given sub-tribe, there might be one such case in a decade.

The Pathan brand of Islam more or less forbids a woman to divorce – while, according to Islam itself, she can. Indeed, when a man divorces a woman in the Mahsud territory, he will insist that no one in the area marries her; she can only marry someone from outside. There have been cases of Mahsud women running away to Waziri villages, and Waziri women to Mahsud villages.

ARRANGED MARRIAGES

In the Mahsud tribe, when a family is interested in their son marrying the daughter of a particular family, they send a basket of fruit to that family's home. If the fruit is accepted, then a couple of women from the man's family will go over to see the girl. If the girl is acceptable, then the marriage is arranged. A comparable practice is followed, with slight modifications, throughout the Tribal Areas.

Although marriage customs vary from tribe to tribe, the one similarity is the tradition of the man paying a bride-price (a sum of money paid to the bride's father). The amount varies according to the prestige of the girl's family as well as the affluence or poverty of the particular area. It is a misconception among outsiders that anyone who can afford it can 'buy' a woman from the Tribal Areas. In fact, the girl's parents give a lot of consideration to the proposal

before they even entertain the womenfolk of the interested household. They take into account such factors as how honourable the man's family is and how well they would be able to look after the girl. Rarely is a girl given to anyone outside the tribe.

I feel that the Pathan practice of the man paying money to the bride's father is far preferable to the custom known as the dowry system, adapted from Hinduism by Muslims of the subcontinent. In the dowry system the bride has to bring a certain amount of money, material objects or jewellery with her. Some poor parents go bankrupt trying to get their daughters married, and many of them grieve when daughters rather than sons are born. The groom's family specifies the type of dowry they want, and the marriage is conditional upon the bride's family being able to meet the demands. Even material objects like air conditioners, a refrigerator, a car, can be specified. I find the dowry system

Women relaxing outdoors in the Orakzai Tirah after finishing their work. These houses are built on the hillside.

141

un-Islamic, materialistic and distasteful. Among the Hindus in India it has caused social problems in certain classes. Occasionally, brides have been pressurized so much by in-laws who felt they had not provided enough dowry that they have committed suicide. In the dowry system a girl is a burden to a family, while in the Pathan, and also Arab, culture, where brides are paid for, a woman is considered an asset.

A 16TH–CENTURY MARRIAGE

It is not only Westerners but also many Pakistanis who believe that the Pathans sell their women to anyone who can afford them. This misconception is well illustrated by an incident that took place in the 1540s on the banks of the Indus among the Niazis. Although it was over 450 years ago, the attitude of the Pathans to their women, and the misunderstanding of the situation by a foreigner, are much the same as they are today. Basically, women in the Tribal Areas have always been treated differently from the way they are treated elsewhere in the subcontinent.

Sher Shah Suri, the great Pathan king of the Suri tribe, had made his nephew, Mubarak Shah, governor of an area along the Indus that was in the hands of the Niazi tribe. On arriving there, Mubarak Shah heard rumours of the beauty of a girl who belonged to a Niazi subtribe, the Sumbhal. Without even seeing her he asked her father, Ahadad Khan, for her hand in marriage. Even though Mubarak Shah's uncle was Sher Shah Suri, Ahadad Khan declined the proposal because Mubarak Shah's mother was a slave.

In a rage Mubarak Shah began a reign of tyranny over the Sumbhals. Eventually a group of Sumbhal elders visited him to explain that since he had grown up in India he was not aware of the Pathan customs. They told him that Pathan women were treated with respect by their men, that they could not be one of a harem, and that if Ahadad's daughter were forcibly married to Mubarak Shah it would be an insult to the whole tribe. Moreover, Mubarak's mother had been a slave. Incensed, Mubarak Shah ordered his soldiers to throw out the delegation – who in turn were so angry at the insult that they slew the guards and executed Mubarak Shah.

Sher Shah Suri then sent my Niazi ancestor, Haibat Khan Niazi, governor of his western empire, to teach the Sumbhals a lesson. They retreated into the mountains, sending word that it was because they did not want to shed Niazi blood (since they were Niazis themselves) that they had not fought him. In return, Haibat Khan Niazi told them that if they came back he would not harm them, as he knew the background to the incident and sympathized with them. When they came to him, however, Haibat Khan Niazi disarmed them, executed a large number of their fighting men and sent some of their women to Sher Shah Suri.

Sher Shah Suri was disgusted by Haibat Khan Niazi's treachery towards his own tribe. He felt that it must be a desperate desire for the throne that drove Haibat Khan Niazi to such an act of betrayal. He also felt, however, that any man capable of such disloyalty to his own tribe could never succeed in his aim of taking the throne. It was thought that Sher Shah Suri was planning to remove Haibat Khan Niazi from his position as governor – but Sher Shah Suri died in an accident before doing so. Ironically, when Haibat Khan Niazi did make a bid for the throne after Sher Shah Suri's death, he was betrayed.

WOMEN'S EDUCATION

The saddest aspect of life for the women of the Tribal Areas is their illiteracy. To begin with, there is hardly any education in the whole of the area. But whatever education there is is for the boys; the girls are left illiterate, as the men don't think it necessary to educate them.

I asked a tribal elder in Waziristan why there isn't more emphasis placed on education in general and on female education in particular. His answer was the standard one that education as a whole had been resisted because it was thought that the British had used it to take away their independence, but that now the elders were changing their attitudes towards education. But, as regards women, he questioned what they could do after being educated. How, he wanted to know, could it change their lives? How would they be better off? I suggested to him that perhaps they would take better care of their children, but I realized it was futile. The tribe's point of view is that within the tribal system it would only cause confusion among the women, and that it is better not to alter the status quo.

The other area where women particularly suffer is when the tribesmen refuse to allow their women to be examined by male doctors. Unfortunately, there are not enough female doctors to serve the Tribal Areas, and as a result women are often deprived of what little medical care is available.

A change is coming, however – as a result of television. Women can watch TV at home and are consequently beginning to educate themselves. My cousin, Jamshed Burki, who was the Political Agent of the Khyber Agency, told me that in Barra the women had actually rebelled. They saw on television how women lived in the rest of Pakistan, while they themselves had such a hard life, and this led them to demand greater luxuries. Perhaps as male education spreads in the Tribal Areas, the women will insist on it too. For, despite their illiteracy, they are strong women who cannot be tyrannized.

CHAPTER 6

Looking Ahead

I FOUND IT SO refreshing to travel round the Tribal Areas, particularly after the naked materialism of the 1980s, which manifested itself in phenomena like the yuppies, whose conversation centred around expensive cars, mortgages and lucrative deals. Perhaps I have romanticized the tribal Pathans somewhat, but I have been heartened to find such high values existing in this day and age. I was impressed by the dignity with which even the poorest man carries himself, his forthrightness and extreme politeness, his awareness of his basic rights and his self-respect. The Pathans' belief in the equality of every man, epitomized in the jirga system, is the essence of democracy. I have never

forgotten what my father said when as a boy I asked him whether we belonged to the middle or upper class. His reply was typically Pathan – that no one was above or below us, some were just more fortunate than others. It was only in the Tribal Areas that I saw what he had said being put into practice.

ABOVE *I hope that, as education increases in the Tribal Areas, the girls will benefit as well as the boys.*

PAGE 144 *With adult franchise the maliks would lose their power but the tribal elders would not. Although voting patterns would change, I believe that the tribal structure would probably not alter.*

PAGE 145 *A class of Burki and Mahsud children being taught at a school in South Waziristan. Education is not given enough emphasis in the Tribal Areas and is consequently seriously inadequate, with a vast potential being wasted.*

The Pathans' refusal to tolerate injustice is the true spirit of Islam. They have shown remarkable courage in standing up to unfairness, and over the centuries they have made many sacrifices to preserve their independence.

The supreme importance of honour in the tribal society has led to the notorious blood feuds. However, the examples I have described in this book are extreme cases, and recounting them here makes them seem a more normal feature of life in the Tribal Areas than they actually are. In reality they occur only rarely. In Karachi there is more crime in a week than there is in a year in the whole of the Tribal Areas.

The Pathans have an incredibly strong faith in Islam, and this gives them an extraordinary amount of will-power. Western observers in Afghanistan, as well

Discussing the coming changes to the Tribal Areas with Afridi elders in a village in the Khyber Pass.

as the Russians, were unable to understand the Mujahideen guerrillas' lack of a fear of death. To them death was preferable to a dishonourable existence. It stemmed from their strong faith and the Islamic concept of jihad, which means standing up to any form of exploitation and injustice (not just colonization but also such circumstances as poverty, for example).

Of course, the combination of a deep faith and a lack of education in general has led to the mullahs (priests) having a disproportionately great influence. In the Qur'an there is no mention of a priesthood, as every Muslim is supposed to read and understand the Qur'an. It is also the duty of every Muslim to spread the word; anyone who is educated can have a better understanding of the Qur'an and can lead the prayers and give Qutba (a lecture on Islam). Hence there is no reason to have a paid clergy except as caretakers of mosques. Some members of the clergy developed into scholars and others led the tribesmen into battle against colonial powers, but there were also instances of members of the clergy being bribed. Recently a Political Agent told me that one of the ways he controls his agency is by bribing a mullah and making him toe the government line.

One of the effects of the general lack of education has been an absence of Ijtihad (discussion on Islam, which is encouraged in the religion). The clergy, consequently, considers it to be its right to interpret Islam, and this can also lead to intolerance towards other religious beliefs or other points of view on Islam. Yet Islam preaches tolerance.

The Pathans have preserved their traditions and way of life with remarkably few changes over the centuries, but some change is inevitable. According to Iqbal, the great philosopher-poet of the subcontinent, 'the only thing permanent in this world is change'. To take just one very visible difference, the traditional Pathan pagri (turban) is no longer the only headgear – the more modern cap is now seen in the less remote areas. In the Khyber Agency, for example, 15 years ago every man wore the pagri, whereas now only one man in ten wears it. A change with much greater implications is that of adult franchise. This is bound to be imposed soon in the Tribal Areas, as the pressure is growing from the younger, more educated members of the tribes. The Pakistan government must formulate a new way of dealing with the tribes rather than follow the outdated British policies.

OPPOSITE ABOVE *Timeless landscape: a shepherd's hut near Manzai, South Waziristan.*

OPPOSITE BELOW *A tribesman surveying the historic Gomal Pass, South Waziristan.*

Television is having a huge impact in the Tribal Areas. Apart from the rapid spread of cricket over the last decade, it has resulted in women beginning to educate themselves, and to ask whether their lives can be made a little easier. Not only television but also the increased wealth coming into the Tribal Areas from Pathans working in Karachi or the Gulf is threatening to introduce materialism into the Pathan value system.

Nevertheless, the tribal Pathans have a deep regard for their tribal customs, traditions and heritage which I particularly admire. No matter how educated or sophisticated a Pathan is, whenever he returns to his homeland he wears his tribal clothes – unlike in the Indian subcontinent, where the elite try to distinguish themselves from the masses by wearing Westernized clothes.

Moreover, the language of pushtu is proudly spoken by everyone in the Tribal Areas. Whenever I was there and the people found I could not speak it fluently, they were disappointed, especially the children. The fact that my ancestors had lived in the plains of Punjab for centuries and had stopped speaking it made no difference – in their opinion every Pathan should speak pushtu. By contrast, the educated Punjabis speak Urdu rather than their native Punjabi language to their children, and the Westernized elite elsewhere in Pakistan often speak English to their children.

The reason the tribesmen resisted British education was their determination

ABOVE *A tribesman wearing a traditional turban.*

OPPOSITE *Youngsters still proudly wear their tribal clothing. They are armed according to their age – this boy carries only a catapult.*

to preserve their independence. They did not want the British to impose a foreign culture on them through their education, as happened in India after 1812, when Lord Macaulay made English the language of the Indian elite. The idea was to create a class that was Indian but would speak, behave and think like Englishmen, and represent the interests of the British in the subcontinent. Jean-Paul Sartre, in his book *The Wretched of the Earth*, writes:

> In the 19th century golden age of colonization we used to bring African, Asian and Latin American pseudo free thinkers to Europe and walk them around Lisbon, Paris, London and Amsterdam. After a few months of having amused them with learning a few gestures, dancing, slight change of accent, modern living and various imitations, we would send them back to their own lands. Upon return these people would recognize themselves as superior races and would assume a mission of power with a loudspeaker, that is, they would parrot to their people what we had taught them. These individuals were not only the colonizers, cream of the crop, but also they were a bridge for transferring our wishes to their native people.

These days in Pakistan, as a result of a hundred years of colonization and currently the Western media dominance, our elite looks upon our own society as backward and tries to distance itself from the masses. Culturally, our educated youth is directionless and confused. Like Kemal Ataturk, we harbour the delusion that the way forward is by aping the Western culture rather than just taking its good points and learning from them. I have been saddened to see the Turks trying so hard to be accepted as what at best will only be secondclass Europeans, instead of taking pride in their great history and developing their culture. We in Pakistan can learn from those aspects of the West that have led to its present technologically advanced state. But we can also learn from the tribal Pathans about self-reliance and self-esteem – which can never develop if we have to depend on foreign handouts for our survival.

It was this independent spirit of the Pathans that was behind the immortal words uttered by the 17th century Pathan poet Khushal Khan Khattak when he resigned from the Moghul army: 'So long as I was an officer I was a servant; the office gone, I am a king.'

Index

Acknowledgements

I would particularly like to thank the following people who helped with the preparation of this book:

My cousin, Jamshed Burki, the leading authority on the Tribal Areas, without whom this book could not have been written

Alison Wormleighton, my editor, without whose help it would have been impossible to finish the book

Professor Akbar Ahmed, Fellow of Selwyn College, Cambridge, Iqbal Fellow of Cambridge University, and author of several books on Muslim societies, including the Pathans, for his comments on the manuscript

Pervez A Khan for his excellent photographs

Fuji Films, Pakistan, who provided all of the film for the photographs

Colonel Rahamzad Khan, Commanding Officer of the Scouts in Wana, for his help in travelling around Waziristan

The Burkis of Kanigoram for their hospitality and for providing an escort around South Waziristan

All the Political Agents and Scouts officers who helped me throughout the Tribal Areas